RAFFAELE MATTIOLI LECTURES

In honour of the memory of Raffaele Mattioli, who was for many years its manager and chairman, Banca Commerciale Italiana has established the Mattioli Fund as a testimony to the continuing survival and influence of his deep interest in economics, the humanities and sciences.

As its first enterprise the Fund has established a series of annual lectures on the history of economic thought, to be called the Raffaele Mattioli Lectures.

In view of the long association between the Università Commerciale Luigi Bocconi and Raffaele Mattioli, who was an active scholar, adviser and member of the governing body of the University, it was decided that the lectures in honour of his memory should be delivered at the University, which together with Banca Commerciale Italiana, has undertaken the task of organising them.

Distinguished academics of all nationalities, researchers and others concerned with economic problems will be invited to take part in this enterprise, in the hope of linking pure historical research with a debate on economic theory and practical policy.

In creating a memorial to the cultural legacy left by Raffaele Mattioli, it is hoped above all that these lectures and the debates to which they give rise will prove a fruitful inspiration and starting point for the development of a tradition of research and academic studies like that already long established in other countries, and that this tradition will flourish thanks to the new partnership between the Università Commerciale Luigi Bocconi and Banca Commerciale Italiana.

PUBLIC CHOICE ANALYSIS
IN HISTORICAL PERSPECTIVE

RAFFAELE MATTIOLI FOUNDATION

Alan Peacock

PUBLIC CHOICE ANALYSIS
IN
HISTORICAL PERSPECTIVE

The right of the
University of Cambridge
to print and sell
all manner of books
was granted by
Henry VIII in 1534.
The University has printed
and published continuously
since 1584.

CAMBRIDGE UNIVERSITY PRESS

CAMBRIDGE
NEW YORK NEW ROCHELLE
MELBOURNE SYDNEY

HJ
132
P43
1992

Published by the Press Syndicate of the University of Cambridge
The Pitt Building, Trumpington Street, Cambridge CB2 1RP
32 East 57th Street, New York, NY 10062, USA
10 Stamford Road, Oakleigh, Melbourne 3166, Australia

Edited by Diego Piacentino

First published 1992

Printed in Italy

Library of Congress Cataloging in Publication Data
Main entry under title:
Public Choice Analysis in Historical Perspective
(Raffaele Mattioli Lectures)
At head of title: Raffaele Mattioli Foundation.
Bibliography.
1. Public Finance – Addresses, essays, lectures.
2. Economic History – Addresses, essays, lectures.

I. Peacock, Alan   II. Raffaele Mattioli Foundation.   III Series
HB 3732.D43   1984   338.9   84-21366

British Library Cataloguing in Publication Data
Peacock, Alan
Public Choice Analysis in Historical Perspective
(Raffaele Mattioli Lectures)
1. Economics
I. Title II. Series
339 HB 172.5
ISBN 0 521 430070

CONTENTS

PREFACE

I am very conscious of the honour done to me in being invited
to deliver the Raffaele Mattioli Lectures, and wish to convey
my warm thanks to the Banca Commerciale Italiana and to the
Bocconi University for allowing me this opportunity to crystallise
some of my views on the bearing of economic thought of the
past on the interpretation of the policy problems of today.

My ideas are presented using the broad brush of the Im-
pressionist. This seems the appropriate technique given the
nature of the theme, the bounds set by the number of lectures and
the occasion of its delivery. I have endeavoured to help the
reader who is interested in following up particular aspects of
my main theme by the provision of fairly copious notes and
references to the work of public choice analysts, past and present, and to some of my own articles and books.

These lectures would never have reached the stage of delivery,
far less the stage of printing, without the kind assistance of several colleagues and officials of the Banca Commerciale Italiana.

I wish to thank, in particular, Drs Bernardo Crippa and An-
tonello Mela of the Bank for the administrative arrangements;
Drs Diego Piacentino and Manfredi La Manna for their pains-
taking editorial input; Professor Ilde Rizzo for guidance in
the choice of Italian economics literature considered in these
lectures; the Discussants – Professors Francesco Forte, Bruno
Frey, Emilio Gerelli, Emilio Giardina, Peter Jackson, Franco
Romani and Vito Tanzi – for the profusion of ideas which will
encourage me to undertake further study of matters that I have
neglected.

Finally, I must single out Professor Sergio Steve for special
mention. I owe him an immense debt over many years for the
inspiration of his ideas and his kindly encouragement.

ALAN PEACOCK

PUBLIC CHOICE ANALYSIS
IN HISTORICAL PERSPECTIVE

The four *Raffaele Mattioli Lectures* were delivered by Alan Peacock at the
Università Commerciale "Luigi Bocconi" in Milano, from 5th to 7th April 1989.

FIRST LECTURE
The Demand for Historical Perspective

1. Introduction

The Italian economist and public figure in whose memory these lectures were founded, regarded the writings of the masters of the past as a source not only of enjoyment but also of inspiration and enlightenment. I am sure that all of us have derived consumption benefits from reading the classics of the past and have our own particular favourites. In the field of public finance and public choice alone, who would not admire the penetrating, terse analysis interlarded with good humour in David Hume's essays, the breadth of vision and style of Smith's analysis of the tasks of government, the way in which Wicksell builds his analysis out of a balanced critique of the work of his forebear and contemporaries, and the audacity of Einaudi's ideas – to mention only a few writers familiar to us all? I am sure also that most of us perceive that there are external economies of production to be derived from even casual reading of the works of our forebears, in the sense that we may believe that our own output of ideas and their application benefit from avoiding what Lionel Robbins in a familiar phrase called "provincialism in time". We all enjoy, I suspect, garnishing our contributions to economic literature with a pithy quotation from "the classics", though a veneer of scholarship must not have us subjected to the charge of misplaced reverence for the past.

I could rest my case for devoting these lectures to a study of the links between past and present writings on public finance and public choice on the inspirational content of the contribution of our forebears. I do not do so, for I have no great discoveries to report, which would differentiate my product from

3

those who have much greater claims to be scholars of our subject. In any case, if I did so, I suspect that I would be doing less than justice to the Mattioli tradition which I take to be the view that the study of the history of economic ideas is an essential part not only of the education but also of the training of an economist, and, what is more, requires professional economists to refer back frequently to the literature of the past. This is a much more difficult case to establish, and, although I have every sympathy with it and believe it applies in my own case, such as it is, I am not sure that I can find completely convincing arguments to support it. However, even if I would find it difficult to accept that the history of economic ideas is an indispensable piece of the equipment of a professional economist, I think that it must be included amongst the list of alternative factors within the combination of factor inputs which produce present-day output of economic ideas and their application to policy questions. I shall go further and argue that the opportunity cost of historical perspective may indeed be lower in the production of ideas about the role of the public sector in the economy, the subject matter of our disciplines, than in other fields of political economy.

In this opening lecture, I shall offer a general survey of the contemporary view of what I shall call "the demand for historical perspective". I shall then develop my case for retaining the history of economic ideas as a significant, if not indispensable, element in the training of specialists in public finance and public choice. I shall consider the question: "is there evidence that 'output' has in any way suffered because of a lack of historical perspective?" Answering that question will provide me with a simple methodology which I shall use in illustrating the value of historical perspective in the analysis of public sector growth, which will form the subject of subsequent lectures.

2. The Fall in the Demand for Historical Perspective

In my professional life, I have witnessed a remarkable shift in the demand curve for historical perspective – to the left. When I was an undergraduate, a course on the history of economic thought was the spinal column of the degree in Political Economy in Scotland and certainly an integral part of the main and specialised courses in economic theory in England. The public recognition of this phenomenon can be gauged by the question put to me by the Chief Education Officer of Scotland when I first became a full Professor in Edinburgh in 1957. He asked me: "and what is your period?" He meant, of course, who were the political economists of the past on whom I claimed to be an authority. My retrospective reply to him, given in my Inaugural Lecture,[1] was "the next ten years and beyond" and a firm statement to the effect that we do not emulate the example of Adam Smith merely by being an authority on what he wrote. My reforming zeal led me to consign the history of economic ideas to a specialised course given by an economist with little interest in research, but in my own defence let it be said that not long afterwards I did appoint a young economist who is now famous for his work in the history of ideas, Donald Winch, though he was also expected to teach international economics! What I did was typical of my generation of younger heads of department. The history of economic ideas appeared to have too high an opportunity cost as an input into the basic training of economists, though it could be taken as an optional course, useful for those who combined economics with more historically or institutionally inclined disciplines such as history and politics. As in many Anglo-Saxon universities, it was feared that it might become a haven for those less gifted in or resistant to mathematics and statistics. At the research level, there were positive dangers perceived in concentrating on the scholastic aspects of the history of ideas, as was pointed out to me at

1. ALAN T. PEACOCK, 'From Political Economy to Economic Science', Inaugural Lecture as Professor of Economic Science, University of Edinburgh, *University of Edinburgh Gazette*, 1957.

the London School of Economics by my colleagues when I considered writing a Ph. D. thesis on the work of von Mangoldt. Scholarly work required roundabout methods of production, yielding returns only in the long term, and uncertain ones at that, in the sense that my peer group would regard scholasticism as a poor substitute for evidence of analytical ability. The personal satisfaction derived from discovering new facts about and presenting new insights into the works of dead men would be bought at the risk of losing promotion, remaining a junior lecturer whilst others were pushing out a stream of articles in major journals and becoming "upwardly mobile". Being poor, married with children and somewhat risk averse, I delayed indulgence in the exploration of the past sufficiently to heed their advice. The clearest evidence of the decline of interest in and the influence of historical perspective in economics may be seen in the comparative growth of articles in economics and public finance journals on the various disciplines. "HET" now comes bottom of the list of the main specialist categories.[1]

I am simply not competent to explain in detail how this remarkable change infected economics principally in Anglo-Saxon countries, and it would take me too far away from my main theme to explore the characteristics of economists' utility functions when it comes to their perception of the factor-mix of what they produce. Two obvious explanations may be briefly mentioned both of which are associated with the perceived obsolescence of ideas from the past as a tool of the trade. The first was the manifest success of mathematical formulation of economic propositions, an activity which, it must be recalled, is as old as economics as a systematic discipline. Claiming attention for one's competence as an economist no longer required extensive knowledge of and commentary on the work of precursors. It is clearly difficult to date the change, and it certainly did not take place simultaneously in countries noted for their contributions to economic thought. If we take public finance, Wicksell, as we have noted, clearly regarded it as necessary to stake his claim to auth-

---

1. See DAVID C. COLANDER and ARJO KLAMER, 'The Making of an Economist', *Journal of Economic Perspectives*, Fall 1987, pp. 95-111, for United States evidence.

ority in economic speculation by extensive quotation from past writers, before presenting his own formulation of the principles of just taxation. His work[1] appeared, significantly enough, in German in 1896, but there is a marked change in the exposition of his follower Lindahl in which his commentary on past writers is consigned to footnotes, though, even in 1919, he writes also in German.[2]

The second explanation lies in the increase in the demand for economic advice as a contribution to the solution of policy problems. It is an intriguing question how far the economic analysis of "market failure" led to the supply of ideas creating its own demand, but the result which was clear enough is that the form of economic advice required economists to teach economic logic to those in charge of policy and to attempt to quantify the influence of policy measures on the appropriate economic variables, such as employment, output and prices. Placed more in the limelight of policy, the economists' skills had to include the classification if not the collection of data, learning how to analyse the data and how to develop economic models which embodied assumptions about the influence of government policy measures. "HET" was simply crowded out by the change in the nature of the economists' product. As I shall demonstrate, the treatment of government solely as a policy mechanism was one of the unfortunate results, a mistake which might have been avoided by an investment in historical perspective.

In my own country, however, the process went much further than the relegation of "HET" to a secondary role in the education and training of economists. In a remarkable book, the British historian J. H. Plumb[3] shows how modern historians have systematically destroyed the past as having some special relevance in defining the role of a particular people or nation and the

1. KNUT WICKSELL, *Finanztheoretische Untersuchungen nebst Darstellung und Kritik des Steuerwesens Schwedens*, Jena: G. Fisher, 1896.

2. ERIK LINDAHL, *Die Gerechtigkeit der Besteuerung: Eine Analyse der Steuerprinzipien auf der Grundlage der Grenznutzentheorie*, Lund: Gleerup und H. Ollson, 1919. The relevant analysis is translated as 'Just Taxation – A Positive Solution', in RICHARD A. MUSGRAVE and ALAN T. PEACOCK, eds., *Classics in the Theory of Public Finance*, London: Macmillan, 1958.

3. See J. H. PLUMB, *The Death of the Past*, London: Macmillan, 1969.

courses of action which will both ensure and sanctify its material and spiritual success. The past, so it has become fashionable to believe, has become an encumbrance in trying to understand the problems of modern society for the descriptions and analysis of past events has been surrounded by myth and dogma. A similar attempt to "kill the past" is associated particularly with the attitude of the famous Cambridge School beginning with Alfred Marshall, although the reasons differed with different members of it. Marshall was a dominant figure who was acutely jealous not only of his contemporaries but of those who may have anticipated his views. He was grudging in his praise of his forebears and extremely selective in his choice of "honourable mentions" of both his precursors and contemporaries. His contemptuous treatment of socialist economics and particularly Marx is almost pathological, and seems to have infected Keynes.[1] He seemed to have made a deliberate attempt to suppress competition from non-British economists by his influence on editorial policy of the *Economic Journal* and was furious, so it has been reported, when he discovered that Edgeworth had adopted the cowardly practice of criticising him by publishing the criticism in an Italian journal! His rationalisation of his wish to ignore the past was that one's time should not be wasted on "the mistakes of dead men"![2] Pigou's work, *A Study in Public Finance*,[3] is practically innocent of references to past work with a notable absence of any discussion of what we would today call public

1. I know that this judgment might be regarded as too sweeping, but see the important article containing the evidence by TERENCE W. HUTCHISON, 'Insularity and Cosmopolitanism in Economic Ideas, 1870-1914', *American Economic Review*, May 1955, pp. 1-16. Hutchison is more charitable than I am and attributes Marshall's refusal to countenance discussion of other schools of thought involving unfamiliar concepts and expressed in other languages as a way of avoiding the "sales resistance" to economic ideas emanating from practical men of affairs whom he desired to influence. In post-Marshallian Cambridge, at least it can be claimed by the "left wing", that they have derived continuous and deep inspiration from the works of Ricardo and Marx.

2. For a detailed examination of Marshall's views on his forebears and contemporaries, see *The Early Economic Writings of Alfred Marshall, 1867-1890*, edited and introduced by JOHN K. WHITAKER, London: Macmillan, 1975, vol. 1, Chapter 1.

3. ARTHUR C. PIGOU, *A Study in Public Finance* (1928), Third edition, London: Macmillan, 1947.

choice problems which had already appeared in the Italian and Swedish literature.[1] Keynes presents a curious paradox. In his earlier writings he specialised in the production of vignettes on such economists as Jevons, Ricardo and Marshall himself which are sympathetic, but his attack on classical macroeconomic theory is wholly misplaced and his search for companionship with "the economic underworld" of Major Douglas, Silvio Gesell and J. A. Hobson verges on the grotesque.[2] In Keynes's case, "cocking a snook" at the past was a fashionable sales technique used by his Bloomsbury friends, such as Lytton Strachey, and clearly not designed to be taken entirely seriously. He was quite capable at looking for allies amongst his forebears on a selective basis, notably in ingratiating himself with his French colleagues by the claim that his views on the rate of interest had an affinity with those of Montesquieu![3] It would be absurd to argue that the upshot of this cavalier treatment of the history of ideas, particularly ideas from other countries, produced some form of intellectual paralysis in Anglo-Saxon thinking. On the contrary, the Ricardian-Marshallian tradition of analysis with its emphasis on problem solving is, as we are all aware, one of the most important contributions to economics. No doubt there has been a parallel neglect of this tradition in other countries, particularly in those countries where analytical relativism held sway, that is to say in countries such as Germany where generalisations in economics were claimed to be conditioned by the problems of a particular era. The fact remains, however, that the Cambridge tradition, which was enormously influential in the field of public finance in Anglo-Saxon countries, was characterised by a distinct

1. Blaug records that Pigou, when asked to review a work on the history of economic thought, replied: "These antiquarian researches have no great attraction for one who finds it difficult enough to read what is now thought on economic problems, without spending time in studying confessedly inadequate solutions that were offered centuries ago". See MARK BLAUG, *Economic Theory in Retrospect*, Fourth edition, Cambridge: Cambridge University Press, 1985, p. 1.

2. See JOHN MAYNARD KEYNES, *The General Theory of Employment, Interest and Money* (1936), reprinted in *The Collected Writings of John Maynard Keynes*, vol. VII, London: Macmillan, 1975, Chapter 23.

3. See KEYNES, 'Preface to the French Edition', in *The General Theory of Employment, Interest, and Money, op. cit.*, p. xxxv.

neglect of governmental institutions as a suitable subject for analysis. Marshall's natural caution led him to be very careful about the claims of economic analysis in identifying policy measures, even before any consideration which might have been given by him to how such measures might be implemented. In the field of public finance, for example, he is noted for his famous proposal that collective satisfaction could be increased if increasing cost industries were taxed and the proceeds used to subsidise decreasing cost industries, but he makes a number of important reservations about the possibility of translating such a proposal into positive action.[1]

The interesting case, naturally, is that of Keynes. He was clearly much more confident about what governments should be doing, as witness his enormous output of policy recommendations culminating in the famous last chapter of the *General Theory*. He had also a great deal of practical experience within government in both World Wars. Yet he was imbued with what public choice theorists, such as Buchanan, Burton and Wagner[2] and latterly Rowley,[3] have labelled the "Harvey Road mentality", kindred intellectual spirits who believed that the United Kingdom should and would be governed by an intellectual aristocracy, namely themselves, who could persuade the public and politicians to follow their prescriptions. This presupposed, in Keynes's case, that functional finance was largely a question of knowing which policy instruments to choose and what their quantitative effects would be on relevant policy variables, such as aggregate expenditure and its components. This approach contains two cardinal errors. It assumed that private sector decision makers reacted purely passively to government measures and were incapable of learning how to adjust their actions. It assumed that even if the behavioural assumptions regarding the

1. See ALFRED MARSHALL, *Principles of Economics* (1890), Ninth (Variorum) edition, Edited by W. CLAUDE GUILLEBAUD, London: Macmillan, 1961, vol. 1, Book v, Chapter XIII.
2. See JAMES M. BUCHANAN, JOHN BURTON and RICHARD E. WAGNER, *The Consequences of Mr. Keynes*, London: Institute of Economic Affairs, 1978.
3. See CHARLES K. ROWLEY, 'John Maynard Keynes and the Attack on Classical Political Economy', in JAMES M. BUCHANAN, CHARLES K. ROWLEY and ROBERT D. TOLLISON, eds., *Deficits*, Oxford: Blackwell, 1987, pp. 115-22.

private sector were realistic, governments could ignore any political feedback from policy measures which were perceived as undesirable by taxpayers-voters.

It is now easily understood why public choice theorists have attacked Keynesian views on the place of the public sector in the economy on positive grounds. Furthermore, normative public choice theory, with its strong emphasis on an individualistic economic philosophy, would add the further objection that the logical consequence of any attempt to implement Keynesian policies would require the institution of dictatorship which would be undesirable in itself.[1]

This illustration raises a big question about the place of the history of economic ideas as an input into the production of new ideas. How can we be sure that if the Cambridge School, to take the example at hand, had been more receptive to an eclectic view of economics, notably in the field of the analysis of the public sector, that they would have avoided what today is regarded as a notable error of omission in the study of policy questions? We have no means of knowing. The use of Marshallian-type partial analysis in the study of bureaucratic behaviour, for instance, might simply have increased their resolve to adopt a patrician stance on political matters, which could be threatened by bureaucratic motivation. Close pre-occupation with past ideas might have, at the margin at any rate, diverted scarce intellectual resources away from development of problem-solving techniques. What we can say is that they established a tradition by which the sanctioning of their policy conclusions did not require any reference to the tastes and preferences of those who elected governments, those who formed governments and those who served governments.

Although public choice theory and the tradition which it champions in the history of ideas has begun to take root amongst Anglo-Saxon, predominantly American, economics, the effect of this on the demand for historical perspective amongst economists

---

1. A view also supported by MILTON FRIEDMAN: see 'Keynes's Political Legacy', in *Keynes's General Theory: Fifty Years On — Relevance and Irrelevance to Modern Times*, London: Institute of Economic Affairs, 1986, pp. 45-55.

has been, so far as I can judge, marginal though perceptive. That being so, I address myself to the main task of this lecture which is to add my mite to attempts to arrest the decline in the study of ideas, like a company faced with a decline in the demand for its product, by informative and, to some extent, persuasive advertising!

3. *The Scope of Public Choice Analysis*

Before I come to the question of the utility of past economic ideas, I had better recall the scope of public choice analysis and the particular part of it on which these lectures are concentrated.

Public choice analysis is the examination of individual and group decision making in the conduct of transactions which, while analogous to those of the market, do not replicate market situations, in which the outcome of those decisions will be a set of prices and outputs. It produces hypotheses about the outcome of these transactions. I have elsewhere identified three major political "markets" in which such hypotheses can be developed though I recognize that public choice analysis can be applied in many other areas, such as international politics and the internal politics of organisations, where bargains are struck without the exchange of money. There is first of all the "primary political market" in which politicians sell policies for votes. The associated theory forms the principal element in public choice theory which is the analysis of the outcome of various forms of voting systems and leading to such influential but contestable propositions as the median voter theorem. Secondly, there is the "policy supply" market in which bureaucrats will offer alternative administrative packages to promote the policy aims of elected governments. The analysis of the outcomes of the demand for and supply of such packages is exemplified in the economic theory of bureaucracy, where current controversy centres on the Niskanen theorem that bureaucrats maximise the size of their budget. The third "market" or set of markets is much less closely integrated with public choice theory and is one which I have tried to develop together with various colleagues. I call it the "policy execution" market. Even in standard public choice modelling, it seems to have been implicitly assumed that those whose actions are affected by policy execution, such as taxpayers, receivers of welfare benefits, industrial and cultural subsidies and suppliers of goods to government, more or less passively adjust to the requirements of the law.[1]

1. Cf. ALAN T. PEACOCK, *The Economic Analysis of Government and Related Themes*, Oxford: Martin Robertson, 1979, Chapter 1.

One should note the strong contrast with the economic theory of regulation where it is assumed that compliance with the law does not produce this result but leads to the "capture" of the regulators by the regulated. I have argued elsewhere that in important regulatory fields, passive adjustment "in reverse" of this kind is not a universal phenomenon and that what is actually observed in the regulation "market" is a bargaining situation between regulators and regulatees. Likewise, I have argued along with Francesco Forte and Martin Ricketts that bargaining is a feature of situations where the government uses the budget as a regulatory device, notably in the fields of tax compliance and the use of subsidies as ways of influencing the decisions of companies and individuals. The associated analysis is akin to the recent use of principal-agent analysis with the government acting as "principal" and the public as "agents" of government.[1]

Like all paradigms, this triangular market system linking individuals in various roles, companies, politicians and bureaucrats is highly simplified. At the same time, I believe that it is a much better approach to the analysis of government than the paradigm derived from the theory of economic policy commonly used in explaining how macro-economic policy operates.

A diagrammatic comparison (see Figure 1, p. 15) of the two systems may help to point the contrast.

So far I have examined the dimensions of positive public choice theory, but its main proponents have also directed their attention at normative aspects of public choice. The central problem of normative theory has been seen as the application of Paretian welfare analysis to situations where political choices form a major element in individual choices, these choices usually being expressed in the form of public goods as additional arguments in the individual welfare function. If markets cannot be established in public goods, then the central problem becomes one of examining which voting systems best approximate to

1. See, successively, ALAN T. PEACOCK and FRANCESCO FORTE, eds., *The Political Economy of Taxation*, Oxford: Blackwell, 1981, Part 1; and ALAN T. PEACOCK *et al.*, *The Regulation Game: How British and West German Companies Bargain with Government*, Oxford: Blackwell, 1984.

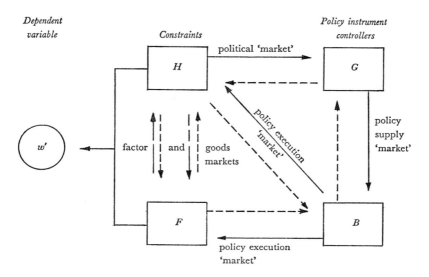

w' = policy outcome (as reflected in objectives, e.g. rate of inflation, employment, etc.)
G = government (vote maximiser)
B = bureaucracy (output maximiser? budget maximiser?)
H = households/voters (utility maximisers)
F = firms (utility maximisers)

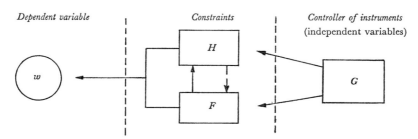

w = welfare function of 'government'
G = 'government' (collective welfare maximiser)
F = 'firms' (profit maximisers)
H = 'households' (utility maximisers)

Figure 1. Policy Paradigms.

Paretian criteria. Thus the "political market", "the policy supply" and "policy execution markets" are treated as a problem of how to eliminate X-inefficiency and allocative inefficiency in the relations between the transactors.

Just as it seems odd to me that Keynes should choose such strange bedfellows from the past, it must seem quite bizarre to Italian colleagues to have Pareto associated with an individualistic, normative theory of public choice, for as you know better than I do, Pareto considered that his criteria for allocative efficiency applied only to the private economy.[1] His views on the appropriate tasks of government and who should have the power to perform them bore little relationship to an individualistic position. Be that as it may, there is no rule that requires that all public choice analysts should be bound to the social decision rules emanating from Paretian welfare economics even if they are individualists. One of the most perceptive positive analyses of the evolution of the system of public finance was presented by Rudolf Goldscheid,[2] a Marxist with strong collectivist leanings. I wrote a book a few years ago with Charles Rowley specifically devoted to an explanation of the profound differences between a Paretian and liberal position on the normative aspects of public choice,[3] emphasising the liberal rejection of the view that all outcomes of democratic voting rules are necessarily desirable, though that does not mean that a liberal need reject the democratic voting rules themselves. This refusal to accept that to be a public choice theorist entails the acceptance of fashionable welfare economics makes what are called "end-state" liberals the true heirs of Classical political economy. I shall illustrate that point in more detail later.

1. For a useful summary of the discussion of this aspect of Pareto's work for the non-Italian reader, see GIOVANNI BUSINO, 'Vilfredo Pareto (1848-1923)', in JOHN EATWELL, MURRAY MILGATE and PETER NEWMAN, eds., *The New Palgrave: A Dictionary of Economics*, London: Macmillan, 1987, vol. 3, pp. 799-804. See also P. HENNIPMAN, 'Wicksell and Pareto: Their Relationship in the Theory of Public Finance', *History of Political Economy*, Spring 1982, pp. 37-64.

2. See RUDOLF GOLDSCHEID, 'A Sociological Approach to Problems of Public Finance', in MUSGRAVE and PEACOCK, eds., *Classics in the Theory of Public Finance*, *op. cit.*, pp. 202-13.

3. See CHARLES K. ROWLEY and ALAN T. PEACOCK, *Welfare Economics: A Liberal Restatement*, London: Martin Robertson, 1975.

16

4. The Contribution of Historical Perspective

I now come to the most difficult part of my self-imposed task, that of trying to "sell" historical perspective, and let me stress once again that this is, at most, informative advertising. No attempt is made to claim that other forms of knowledge are "worthless substitutes".

A useful point of departure might be to view the way in which economists spend their day, concentrating on those who view their task as adding to the stock of knowledge.

We would find that a large proportion of the profession, including those concerned with public choice problems, would consider that new insights into the way the economic system, including government, works are useful but not much more than preliminary spadework before formulating testable hypotheses. In line with the natural sciences, the end-purpose of these tasks is to predict movements in economic variables and to suggest ways in which these variables may be controlled, not necessarily but certainly frequently, by government. As McCloskey puts it, "the official methodology of economists is modernist" by which is meant, broadly speaking, that it is "an amalgam of logical positivism, behaviourism, operationalism, and the hypothetico-deductive model of science".[1]

Let me, for the moment, accept this methodological position at its face value. It suggests no place for the study of the history of economic ideas, though some pedagogic returns may be garnered from showing up the crudity of nineteenth century model building and testing. Thus it is not unknown for economists to impress their peers by their powers of transforming these crude attempts into elegant modernist formulations, rather like modern composers of music who "realise" works of the past and in the course of the transformation into modern idioms produce new creations. However, techniques of hypotheses, formulation and testing are not in themselves the sources of hypotheses, though they may suggest ways in which hypotheses under scrutiny might be extended or modified.

1. DONALD N. McCLOSKEY, 'The Rhetoric of Economics', *Journal of Economic Literature*, June 1983, p. 484.

There are several different ways by which an economist arrives at original insights which are recognized as such by his colleagues and even by the world outside. The incentive to seek solutions to a particular problem is often derived from a strong political or social concern and even commitment which, despite professional contempt for "dirtying one's hands with politics", seems to be as legitimate a motive as trying to impress one's peer group. The proposed solutions may be arrived at by close observation of the world around us, by introspection, by intellectual discussion, in short by personal gifts and dispositions which are quite independent of conventional technical skills.

If I am right in claiming that the inspirational sources of insights which lead to the formation of original hypotheses may be many and varied, then this alone makes a case for studying the history of economic ideas, and particularly those representing a different tradition from the one dominating one's own thinking. The effect is rather like that of taking a holiday in what one would regard as an exotic place, but where one is careful to shed one's prejudices about local rules and customs. Observing how another people, or in our case another generation of *confrères*, identify problems which they consider important, how they analyse them and what intellectual and practical solutions they propose may help to generate a new perspective. I hope to demonstrate this to be particularly true in the case of public choice theory.

However, the modernist point of view, as you know, has been under strong attack. There are strong disagreements amongst us not so much about how economic reasoning should be conducted but about the canons applying to the construction of economic models. Models are claimed to be metaphors rather than representations of interconnected parts of an observable reality. Following the philosopher C. S. Lewis, McCloskey goes so far as to argue that an economist who talks "literally" about the demand curve, the national income or the stability of the economy is engaging in "mere syntax".[1] Metaphors can be useful but one must concede that public finance and fiscal policy

1. *Ibid.*, p. 502.

have suffered very badly from metaphors derived from biological and engineering systems in which are embodied very naive ideas about "control mechanisms" within the systems which can be used to "steer" the "system" into some "desired" direction. This has led to a crass oversimplification of the analysis of how governments actually operate, how they could operate, and how they "ought" to operate. I need hardly pile on the agony of reappraisal by reference to the major disputes about the validity of econometric testing, to the pretensions of economic forecasters, to the morality of selling conditional projections as forecasts. It is transparently obvious that we can no longer claim that economics is proceeding *gradum ad parnassum* with the prospect that predictions and therefore the effects of government control will become ever more certain. We have to think twice before consigning our forebears to permanent occupation of what Schumpeter called "the lumber room", though he was careful to stress that visits to it could be made with profit provided one did not stay too long ! One wonders whether Schumpeter ever speculated on how often after his time his own ideas would be taken out and dusted.

When a discipline like economics slips what it believes to be safe moorings, the consideration of what to do forces us to reappraise other approaches which have been discarded or neglected, and which might lead us back to a safer anchorage – you will note how all-pervading is the use of metaphor in that statement ! The most striking example of this has been the revival of interest in the Austrian School. This has gone much further than a ritualistic genuflexion in the direction of its founders. The complete methodology of subjectivism has been deployed to attack the central concept of modernism – the test of predictability. So far its modern adherents have produced no revolutions in our thinking on positive public choice theory, possibly because writers such as Sax and Wieser wrote work which was in close conformity with the contemporaneous interest in applying marginal utility analysis to the functions of the state. The contribution has been of a cautionary nature, for example, in showing how the unknowability of the future destroys the validity of instructions to managers of public enterprise based on marginal cost pricing, particularly in collectivist societies. Another important example lies in the destruction wrought on any government policy which rests on the assumption that consumer preferences are both known and stable.[1] The central point remains. Those who have sought inspiration in Austrian thinking could not have found their moorings without the guiding stars of Böhm-Bawerk, Menger and von Mises. I must justify my "essay in persuasion" by more specific reference to public choice analysis. I hope that no-one will take it amiss if I refer to the influence of historical perspective on my own thinking.

1. The lack of attention to the dynamic process of the market, which the Austrians derived from Adam Smith's doctrine of the Invisible Hand, has led to the proliferation of a misunderstanding by economists – both Cambridge-connected – of the eminence of Hahn and Sen concerning the efficacy of market forces. They have wrongly assumed that the "competitive ideal" is synonymous with a static general equilibrium position in which there is no incentive for further change. On the contrary, the Smithian and Austrian conception of an ideal economic system is based on the ability of the market to produce adjustment to change, including changes in taste. For a full analysis of this historical error, and its implications for attitudes to economic policy, see NORMAN P. BARRY, *The Invisible Hand in Economics and Politics: A Study in the Two Conflicting Explanations of Society, End States and Processes,* London: Institute of Economic Affairs, 1988.

5. A Personal View of Historical Perspective

When in 1951 I was put in charge of the teaching of the economics of public finance at the London School of Economics at the tender age of 29 I suppose I was competent to discourse on the social accounting of public finance, fiscal and social policy in a macro-economic context, and on the more traditional views of shifting and incidence which were regarded as an application of standard micro-economic theory. If there was a co-ordinating feature in the pedagogy of public finance, it lay in the treatment of government as a separate, coherent entity – a "unitary being" in Pigou's famous assumption – actively engaged in influencing the actions of firms and households through various budgetary measures. The reactions of firms and households were encapsulated in changes in price and output or in leisure, saving and work and in Keynesian macro-economic models in changes in aggregate expenditure and its components. The passive nature of these reactions is symbolised by the prevalence of period analysis in which lagged functions are displayed and no learning process is embodied. This co-ordination did not as yet extend to the specification of a government welfare function in which the arguments were clearly delineated, though writers such as Richard Musgrave and Bent Hansen were turning their minds to the problem of integrating the theory of economic policy with fiscal policy. I cannot say that I lost any sleep over pedagogical problems for I was more at home in the macro-economics of public finance than in micro-economics, which may partly be explained by the fact that the former – though I and many others were much mistaken in this – seemed to produce concrete results which could be readily applied to policy. I was however puzzled by the fact that attempts to develop a normative system of public finance were based on the application of utilitarian theory of some form or another, but only to taxation, which meant implicitly accepting that government expenditure played no part in the utility functions of individuals. A further puzzle was that Paretian welfare economics of the Kaldor/Hicks variety had nothing to say about individual choice and the allocation of resources between the public and the private sector.

Two chance events altered my whole conception of the framework of public finance. I had been recruited by the International Economic Association to the Editorial Board of *International Economic Papers* in the mistaken belief that as I knew some German and French and rudimentary Italian I would be qualified to identify historical and contemporary articles in these languages which would be sources of interest and possibly inspiration to economists who confined their study to work in English. Helped by correspondents in mainly European countries, my fellow editors and I made an extensive literature trawl which turned me at least not only into a broker in the translation market but also into a much more avid reader of Continental literature. My first "find" had been an article of Lindahl[1] in a once-well-known survey of contemporary economic thought in which he defended his earlier and now much more famous *Gerechtigkeit der Besteuerung*.[2] I only found one economist in the United Kingdom who had read the Swedish literature and that was Brinley Thomas who had come across it when studying in Berlin in the 1930s, and he encouraged me to master it. The trail led naturally from Lindahl to Wicksell and to those whom Wicksell discussed and criticised, including Wagner and Mazzola. It was a sore temptation not to renew my intention to become a scholar and to regard the history of ideas as my final product. I had a trial run by writing (in 1953) an article in a French journal[3] mainly on Lindahl's and Wicksell's work and by preparing a paper on the theory of public goods for Lionel Robbins' seminar.

I might have written a text on the theory of public expenditure based on these writers but for a second event. On my first visit, in 1953, to the United States, I encountered Richard Musgrave who sat me down to read the first draft of his justly famous

1. See ERIK LINDAHL, 'Einige strittige Fragen der Steuertheorie', in HANS MAYER, ed., *Die Wirtshaftstheorie der Gegenwart*, vol. IV, Vienna: Springer, 1928, pp. 282-304. An abridged English translation by ELIZABETH HENDERSON is to be found in MUSGRAVE and PEACOCK, eds., *Classics in the Theory of Public Finance, op. cit.*, pp. 214-32.

2. *Op. cit.*

3. See ALAN T. PEACOCK, 'Sur la théorie des dépenses publiques', *Économie appliquée*, April-June 1953, pp. 427-45.

The Theory of Public Finance.[1] I cannot think of a better advertisement for my contention that the history of ideas has a substantial part to play in innovations in public finance. His rehabilitation of public goods theory changed the whole direction of discourse on the economics of public finance. I had been anticipated by a better man and, even with freedom of entry into the business, I was not disposed to compete. One further result of the visit was the discovery of a mutual desire to make available translations of the classical works in traditional theory and I was highly satisfied with collusion rather than competition. Our *Classics in the Theory of Public Finance*[2] has been a somewhat unexpected success: has been reprinted twice and has appeared in paperback editions. I attribute this to the fact that it provided an orientation towards the public goods problem which could not then be derived from Keynesian-dominated discussion of the role of the public sector. It revealed that the choice of tax and expenditure policies could only be derived from clearly defined value systems, one of the notable contributions of Italian writers. Insofar as economists had been content to use Paretian welfare economics as a value framework, it faced them with having to turn their attention to the role of the individual consumer in the choice of goods and services provided by government. If the consumer was the best judge of his interests, what reasons were there for not assigning to him the right to make that choice? This is not a simple question to answer, but *Classics* provided a checklist of approaches to an answer which has had considerable influence on the contemporary literature on the theory of social choice.

Close involvement in the process of increasing the supply of classical material generated my own demand for its use. I was asked by the National Bureau of Economic Research, New York, to write a companion study to Moses Abramovitz's *Growth of Public Employment in Great Britain* which appeared in 1957.[3] This would be primarily an attempt to produce a consistent

---

1. See RICHARD A. MUSGRAVE, *The Theory of Public Finance*, New York: McGraw-Hill, 1959.

2. MUSGRAVE and PEACOCK, eds., *Classics in the Theory of Public Finance*, op. cit.

3. MOSES ABRAMOVITZ and VERA F. ELIASBERG, *The Growth of Public Employment in Great Britain*, Princeton: Princeton University Press, 1957.

series of national accounting statistics for government transactions covering a period from before the First World War until the 1950s. It was a daunting task for there were practically no precedents to follow which conformed with the much stricter canons of statistical arrangement which had been laid down by the national income statisticians. If that was not bad enough, the only way of collecting data for the pre-First World War period was to go through the Finance Accounts of Government and reclassify every item. As the statistical work reached the stage where it was as complete as it was ever likely to be, the question arose about how it should be presented and interpreted. There was no other requirement than to present the raw data and to tabulate it in a digestible form. By this time I was rather bored with being once again, as in *Classics*, one of the supervisors of a mining operation where the raw materials would be used by others to produce more glamorous finished products. By great good fortune, Jack Wiseman had joined me in the teaching of public finance and thus began some years of creative tension which neither of us is ever likely to forget.

Recruited as a co-author, he and I began almost day-to-day discussion as to how we could make the pictures tell a story by examining the determinants of the size and structure of the public sector. There is now a well-established procedure for doing this, which I shall consider in critical fashion in my next lecture. For us, there was certainly nothing in the contemporary literature although both Ursula Hicks and Richard Musgrave had remarked upon the influence of changes in economic and social structure on the public finances, including the acceleration of change during wars, as causal factors. Our problem is highlighted by considering contemporaneous attempts to embody the public sector in models of economic growth.

One would have imagined that a study of the process of economic growth would require some consideration of the influence of the public sector on the supply of and demand for resources. However, whereas macro-growth model builders were confident about how to embody determinants of private investment and consumption into aggregate investment and consumption functions, they understandably fought shy of producing a similar function which would have to encapsulate the behaviour of the political system.

The simple way round this difficulty was to ignore it. Domar, for example, assumed government away altogether on the grounds that this was "the most convenient" treatment, "and such a treatment of a troublesome factor is richly supported by precedents in economic theory".[1] This hardly seemed sufficient reason for ignoring a sector which commonly absorbed one-quarter of total annual output of resources. The public sector had to be incorporated somehow, and that could most easily be done if the purpose of the model was to offer prescriptions to government about the amount and composition of taxation and expenditure which would achieve some given growth objective or minimise fluctuations through time.

Such an approach which, incidentally, gave further support to the idea that the government could or should be placed in the position of "fine tuning" the economy, gave little comfort to anyone trying to study the actual determinants of the growth of the public sector, and who was at least aware that what governments actually do could not be divorced from the system which determined how governments were chosen and why they were chosen.

This is what led Jack Wiseman and myself to examine more closely a literature in public finance which had hardly penetrated the footnotes of advanced Anglo-Saxon texts and where the knowledge acquired in preparing *Classics* came in extremely useful. We built our study round a discussion of Wagner's Law, so that we were led back to the end of the nineteenth century. I shall only make two observations on this tribute to our intellectual heritage. The first is that in my ignorance I was unaware of the Italian discussion which goes back to Augusto Graziani and Sitta from whom one might have derived a similar stimulus, and there are other writers, notably Jens Jessen, who pre-echoed our ideas on the "displacement effect" in the observed growth in public expenditure. The second remark concerns Wagner. I think that

---

1. Evsey D. Domar, *Essays in the Theory of Economic Growth,* New York: Oxford University Press, 1957, p. 20.

we can claim to have led the modern revival of interest in his work at least in Anglo-Saxon countries.[1] Over twenty five years later, I suspect that Wagner has many more references in the Social Sciences Citation Index in contemporary literature than we do. What better evidence is required of the potency of an older generation than the fact that his modern sponsors cannot even compete with him in professional attention!

---

[1]. See ALAN T. PEACOCK and JACK WISEMAN, *The Growth of Public Expenditure in the United Kingdom*, Princeton: Princeton University Press, and Oxford: Oxford University Press, 1961; Revised edition, London: Allen and Unwin, 1967, Chapter 2.

6. Concluding Remarks

Let me finish this lecture where I began by emphasising that I do not want to run into the danger of overstating my case. Just as there are many ways of peeling an orange, and many different types of orange to be peeled, the range of products which economists produce is wide and consequently different products, to be efficiently produced, require different input mixes. Though some economists stick to the production of the same type of product all their professional lives, others move from one line of production to another and even back again. Therefore, the interest in the history of ideas as part of the input mix can vary from one product to another and in the case of the individual from one period of professional life to another. I am tempted to go further and to argue that anyone interested in understanding how the economic role of the state is to be analysed and prescribed cannot avoid the study of the history of ideas, but I would prefer to offer you some more examples of the refreshing effect of "visits to the lumber room" before essaying a final judgment. For the moment I would rest my case by saying that in the "further particulars" offered to applicants of positions as academic study of public finance I would like the sentence included that "a knowledge of the history of economic ideas is desirable if not essential".

SECOND LECTURE
Public Choice and the Analysis of Public Sector Growth

1. Introduction. – 2. Studying Public Sector Growth. – 3. The Past as Prologue. – 4. The Stimulus to Present Thinking. – 5. Summary and Conclusions.

1. Introduction

I wish to take as the first illustration of my theme the analysis of public sector growth which, in the course of the last twenty years, has been closely integrated with public choice analysis. But looking forward to later analysis as well as back to my basic thesis, I would like to combine my analytical with my policy interests. To repeat a quotation from Bentham which expresses my position, "it is a vain and false philosophy which conceives its dignity to be debased by use".[1] Whatever satisfaction is gained from the privileges and pleasures of being able to pursue academic studies, I am equally interested in finding out whether the study of the growth of government can teach us anything about the reassessment of the role of government which has occupied the attentions of policymakers in Western industrial nations for several years now.

I hope that I may be forgiven if I do not spend time on discussing such matters as the definition of government employed in studying its growth, the problems which arise in choosing appropriate indicators of growth and the presentation of the facts of growth once appropriate definitions and statistical measures have been identified. These are important preliminary matters which have exercised the skills of many analysts in what has become itself a growth industry.[2] I shall only refer to them if they have a bearing on my general argument. Perhaps one

---

1. JEREMY BENTHAM, 'The Philosophy of Economic Science', in *Jeremy Bentham's Economic Writings*, edited by W. STARK, vol. 1, London: Allen and Unwin, 1952, p. 2.

2. For a useful commentary on such matters, see JOHAN A. LYBECK, *The Growth of Government in Developed Economies*, Aldershot: Gower, 1986, Chapter 3.

preliminary comment on definitions may be helpful. There is a tendency in much of the analytical literature to concentrate on the public finances, particularly in analysing differences between countries. I shall do the same, but there will be times when it is as well to remind ourselves that the definition of the public sector can be extended to cover public enterprises. Indeed, whereas there has been much controversy surrounding the Peacock-Wiseman thesis about the influence of wars and social disturbances on the growth of government, the statistical tests used by critics have generally ignored the fact that we included public enterprises in our definition of government. Latterly, the important point has been made by Bruno Frey[1] that if we are attempting to measure the growing influence of government on the economy through trends in government expenditure and taxation, we must not ignore the importance of use by government of all forms of regulatory devices, even if devising an indicator of regulatory growth may be very difficult.

I shall begin by offering a conspectus of the approaches to the study of government growth. I shall then single out the public choice approach and justify the attention I shall pay to it rather than to other approaches.

1. See BRUNO S. FREY, 'Are there Natural Limits to the Growth of Government?', in FRANCESCO FORTE and ALAN T. PEACOCK, eds., *Public Expenditure and Government Growth*, Oxford: Blackwell, 1985, pp. 101-18.

2. Studying Public Sector Growth

How does one approach the study of public sector growth? Let me explain it in a rather naive way. Imagine that you are commissioned to write the history of your own university or firm covering a century. As an economist or social scientist you would almost certainly not be content with simple description of its growth. At the very least you would pick out some statistical indicators such as growth in revenue, expenditure, employment and the change in product "mix". You would almost certainly be tempted into analysing the causes of the changes in the fortunes of your organisation. You would view the influences on the decisions of the firm's management. Broadly speaking, these could be classified in conventional fashion into changes in demand conditions (and the extent to which these might have been influenced by the firm's marketing decisions) and changes in supply conditions (which again might be classified into those within its control such as in-house changes in technology, and "external factors" beyond its control such as raw material prices). You might be tempted further into showing how the firm's decisions conformed to the kind of utility function associated with the type of organisation and even into identifying when in the course of the history of the organisation, the utility function changed or its parameters altered as a result of some change in its power structure.

One thing is practically certain about the conclusion of your investigation. The relative importance of the causal influences would vary through time. It would be reckless indeed to try to reduce the phenomenon of dynamic change to a simple supply and demand diagram with shifting supply and demand curves, except as a primitive description of what had happened and within a limited period of time, for market form and the product itself would be subject to continuous mutation.

Consider now the study of the growth of the public sector as it has developed historically. The late nineteenth century view, represented by Adolph Wagner and the Italian writers Graziani and Sitta,[1] accorded well with the doctrine of comparative advantage. With the growth of the industrial economy a complementary demand was set up, alongside industrial and manufacturing expansion, for transport and communication services, energy and waste disposal. It was commonly claimed at the time that central and local governments had a comparative advantage in providing such services. It is a view which is capable of development into a more general, all-embracing hypothesis which recognises that comparative advantage is subject to change. For example, George Stigler has used it to attack the Keynesian thesis that politicians are the slaves of defunct economists of which there is a curious contemporary echo in the work of Milton Friedman.[2] Stigler argues:

... the hypothesis is that the propensity to use the state is like the propensity to use coal: we use coal when it is the most efficient resource with which to heat our houses and power our factories. Similarly we use the state to build our roads or tax our consumers when the state is the most efficient way to reach those goals ... When the conditions of society dictate little use of the state, the economy will be characterised as *laissez-faire*. When the conditions of society dictate much use of the state, the economy will be called collectivistic ... To explain how society moves from one of these regimes to the other, one does not look (primarily) to intellectual currents: rather, the explanation will lie chiefly in the changing scope for governmental action as the structure of the economy changes.[3]

It is of interest that a perspicacious writer such as Stigler should have generalised an idea which can be derived from nineteenth century writers though, uncharacteristically, he does not specify its derivation. However, there are a series of immediate

---

1. See ADOLPH A. G. WAGNER, 'Three Extracts on Public Finance', in MUSGRAVE and PEACOCK, eds., *Classics in the Theory of Public Finance, op. cit.,* pp. 1-15. Also, AUGUSTO GRAZIANI, 'Intorno all'aumento progressivo delle spese pubbliche', in *Memorie della Regia Accademia di Scienze,* Modena, 1887, pp. 251-327; and P. SITTA, *L'aumento progressivo delle spese pubbliche,* Ferrara, 1893.

2. MILTON and ROSE FRIEDMAN, *Free to Choose,* New York: Harcourt Brace Jovanovich, 1980, p. 285.

3. GEORGE J. STIGLER, *The Regularities of Regulation,* Edinburgh: David Hume Institute, 1986, pp. 3-4.

questions which require an answer if the idea is to have at least an interpretative value.

How far are these demands for government action formulated and transmitted to government and who transmits them? What relation is there, if any, between the precise benefits sought from "buyers" and the "prices" paid for these benefits? What guarantee is there that the "messages" will be understood and what motive is there for government to act upon them? Why should it be assumed that the government is and will remain the sole supplier of the products demanded?

Clearly, any hypothesis about government growth has to embody asumptions about the political decision-making process, and, as Stigler himself acknowledges, a thesis of government growth which postulates the possibility of a cyclical pattern of government intervention, runs up against the problem that political institutions are themselves influenced by the underlying economic and social structure. Useful though it may be, to pursue the analogy with a study of the changing demand and supply conditions as a method for interpreting the historical development of a firm or other economic institution, it is already fraying at the edges, but analogies are useful if only to point towards differences. One might add parenthetically that one of the great traditions in Italian public finance has been to explore the characteristics of the political choice mechanism and how different mechanisms will affect the outcome of the "bargains" struck between citizens and the state.[1]

None of the writers so far referred to had the intention of doing much more than to emphasise that governments were perceived to have a positive function in the development of the economy,

---

1. On the earlier writings representing this tradition, see in particular JAMES M. BUCHANAN, *Public Finance in Democratic Process: Fiscal Institutions and Individual Choice*, Chapel Hill, N.C.: University of North Carolina Press, 1967, Chapter 7. For recent examples, see particularly: SERGIO STEVE, 'Conclusioni', in EMILIO GERELLI e FRANCO REVIGLIO, eds., *Per una politica della spesa pubblica in Italia*, Milano: Angeli, 1978, pp. 223-31; FRANCESCO FORTE and EMILIO GIARDINA, 'The Crisis of the Fiscal State', in KARL W. ROSKAMP and FRANCESCO FORTE, eds., *Reforms of Tax Systems*, Detroit, Mi.: Wayne State University Press, 1981, pp. 1-9; FRANCO ROMANI, 'Crisi dello stato democratico? Alcune riflessioni sulle finanze pubbliche italiane negli Anni Settanta', in *Saggi su: L'economia italiana negli Anni Settanta, Note Economiche*, Nos. 5-6, 1980, pp. 51-71.

and as perceived by private interest groups, notably industrial pressure groups. In contrast the prevailing Anglo-Saxon idea was that most government expenditure was "onerous", and it was left to some "enlightened" fiscal authority to determine how community "sacrifice" resulting from the transfer of resources[1] was to be minimised. The quantification of the causes of growth and any associated predictions were not contemplated, other than in a rather casual way. Thus, whereas Wagner is saddled with the hypothesis that G/GDP would continue to increase, and, as we have seen, inspired many writers both to interpret, sometimes reinterpret, and test this hypothesis, he was careful to point out that

[t]here is . . . a proportion between public expenditure and national income which may not be permanently overstepped . . . there must be some sort of balance in the individual's outlays for the satisfaction of his various needs. For in the last resort, the State's fiscal requirements covered by taxation figure as expenditure in the household budget of the private citizen.[2]

It is just as well that any prediction was not based solely on the "comparative advantage" hypothesis otherwise it would have been very difficult to explain the growth of social expenditure undertaken by government, and notably the growth in transfers (other than interest on the public debt). This is not to deny that investment in human capital, and therefore in education and health services, was not being considered as an important factor in economic growth; such ideas are as old as systematic economic thinking. What is more questionable is whether government has a comparative advantage in producing them.

It is here that we can introduce the second strand in the discussion of "demand influences" on government growth. Today it is called "the demand for redistribution"[3] and initially we shall explore this concept with reference to vertical redistribution.

---

1. This view still dominates the position of such a prominent analyst as Pigou in the 1940s. See PIGOU, *A Study in Public Finance, op. cit.,* Chapter III, para. 5.

2. WAGNER, 'Three Extracts on Public Finance', *op. cit.,* p. 8.

3. See, for example, SAM PELTZMAN, 'The Growth of Government', *Journal of Law and Economics*, October 1980, pp. 209-87.

The first characteristic of this view is the explicit introduction of voters as the main driving force in the political decision-making system but as a positive factor and not simply as a normative imperative. The discussion of the outcome of alternative voting systems goes back to the eighteenth century but spawned a literature primarily designed to identify "efficient" or "just" decisions; and the pioneering work of Wicksell is directed towards the same end. The voter and combinations of voters in political parties or interest groups exercising tangible political influence do not come into their own, with one notable exception which I shall examine closely, until the early work of Lindahl,[1] though the Classical economists recognised very clearly how potent that force could be. At first sight, a "taste for income redistribution" suggests a re-drawing of the voter welfare function along neo-Paretian lines[2] to reflect positive utility derived by the rich from transferring resources to the poor. Philanthropy is certainly an established fact and it could also be argued that the state role in furthering the redistribution aims of the "rich" is designed to get round the "free rider" problem, for a voluntary system of transfers might break down because of prohibitive transaction costs between the "rich" and because the "rich" who wished to avoid their "obligations" could avoid subscribing to "charity contracts" unless they were compulsorily enforced. However, this argument presupposes that the motive force for redistribution would come from agreements amongst the rich in which the "poor" would have no part. In other words it assumes a political franchise limited only to those who confer the benefits and not to those who receive them. Once we enter a world in which the franchise is universal and voter participation is not so skewed that the "poor" are simply content to sanction the decisions of the "rich", then the "demand for redistribution" can be derived from a much simpler model of human behaviour. This is the de Tocqueville model which I shall consider in detail later. At this

1. In his justly famous work *Die Gerechtigkeit der Besteuerung, op. cit.*
2. A large literature on the subject has spawned from HAROLD M. HOCHMAN and JAMES R. RODGERS, 'Pareto Optimal Income Redistribution', *American Economic Review*, September 1969, pp. 542-57, and the early commentaries by RICHARD A. MUSGRAVE and ROBERT S. GOLDFARB, same *Review*, December 1970, pp. 991-9.

35

juncture, let me just mention its basic essentials. Assume that the political decision rule is that of simple majority, that the initial income distribution is such that the median income level of voters is below the average income of voters, and that the franchise is universal. Assume that everyone votes for a personal income level, after redistribution by the state, which increases his real income. Initially, the majority of voters would gain from redistribution, and the lower the median income relative to the mean, the more the process of redistribution would continue. However, as the average post-redistribution income approaches the post-redistribution median income, the less opportunity exists for gains through redistribution to take place. In short, here we have an influence on the growth of public transfers which suggests not only that the growth may be positive, under certain conditions which are recognisably in accordance with the facts, but also suggests that there could be a finite limit to that growth.

I would be the first to agree that this new twist to the study of the "effective demand" for government expenditure growth is perhaps more intriguing rather than illuminating and raises many questions. Why does so little redistribution appear to occur, insofar as redistribution is capable of measurement? How do we account for the relative proportions of social expenditure between "real" and money transfers? The store of loose ends to be tied up could be extended much further. Sufficient has been said to point again in the direction of the differences between exchange relationships in ordinary markets and in the "political market". One might view this "market for redistribution" as analogous to a market in which the producer employs price discrimination between different classes of "buyers", but only in a formal sense. As soon as we try to press the analogy further, we are forced to recognise the importance of acquiring knowledge about the "objective function" of "the government", and, without detailed enquiry, it is clear that the motive for price discrimination has nothing to do with the maximising of profit by the state, once it is accepted that its actions are markedly influenced by a voting system. Moreover, a model of pure public choice where decisions are taken by what amounts to referenda may be a useful point of departure to generate an understanding of the link between voter motivation, but its translation into influence on government actions ignores the fact that the transaction costs to voters of running government like a small town meeting are so prohibitive that the logic alone of public choice theory would require that the kinds of policies voters will wish to support demand some form of representative government. Furthermore, I need hardly point out to an Italian audience that a "contractarian" approach to the study of government, while it may form the basis for a normative theory of government, gives us little guidance on how political institutions may actually be established, and the changing role and influence government may have on the growth in its activities. Indeed, it can be highly misleading as a general indication of the historical development of government where the franchise has rarely if ever been the spontaneous result of some contractual agreement amongst equals, but a reluctant concession by aristocracies to the growing economic power of the "lower orders". David Hume, that great inspirer of public choice theorists, did not make this mistake. Writing of the idea of a social contract he drew a firm distinction between its justification and its supposed origin:

[m]y intention here is not to exclude the consent of the people from being one just foundation of government where it has place. It is surely the best and most sacred of any. I only pretend that it has very seldom had place in any degree, and never almost in its full extent. And that therefore some other foundation of government must also be admitted.[1]

I shall return to the question of the role of the franchise in the growth of government at various later stages but before moving, as our argument requires, to consider the supply conditions attached to government services, it should also be noted that, as government grows, it grows in complexity, in the sense that the individual is confronted with a growing array of measures, both on the tax and expenditure side of the budget,

---

1. DAVID HUME, 'Of the Original Contract' (1748), reproduced in *Essays, Moral, Political and Literary*, edited by EUGENE MILLER, Indianapolis, In.: Liberty Classics, 1985, p. 474.

which affect his or her welfare, and which may not be capable of clear interpretation. The individual cannot monitor the effect on his welfare by the simple and infrequent process of voting, but must have recourse to other instruments of political participation.[1] The incentive to identify oneself with an interest group, to employ "agents" to bargain with government and even to adopt modes of action of doubtful legality is increased.[2] Therefore, to confine the study of demand pressures on government to the political market, in the narrow sense of the voting in of governments in power, is to ignore other methods by which individual tastes and preferences for government goods and services and their finance may be expressed. Hence the emphasis in my first lecture on the importance of the bargaining relationship between government and the citizen.

It must be true that a necessary condition for expansion of G/GDP in a modern Western-type democracy is voter support, just as a necessary condition for a firm to survive and expand must be demand for its products. But demand cannot be a sufficient condition. There is certainly a presumption that some part of the explanation of the growth of government must lie with supply conditions. In the short run, a monopoly supplier can exercise control over market conditions through its control of price, which implies the absence of alternative sources of supply, but in the longer run firms may be taken over and the new shareholders can vote the management out of office. New entrants using process and product innovations may erode their market share. Centralised governments at least have more extensive powers, even though such governments may be voted out of office and replaced, just as with a take-over in business. But whichever government is in power, it can normally prevent competition in the "government business", and it can use its powers of compulsion. It can incur debt to finance further expansion, given the assurance that it is permitted to tax future

1. The seminal work on this question is ALBERT BRETON, *The Economic Theory of Representative Government*, London: Macmillan, 1974.
2. For a fuller discussion of this question with particular reference to the tax system, see ALAN T. PEACOCK and FRANCESCO FORTE, eds., *The Political Economy of Taxation, op. cit.*, 1981, Chapter 2.

generations. An interesting case is state pension provision where the voting and working population of today can support improved pensions for themselves in the future without having to make a contract with those who will have to pay for them – future generations of voters – though this argument rests on the assumption that future generations will honour past "obligations".

The importance of the monopoly power of government lies less in the control given over the pattern of expenditure and more in its efficiency. With no alternative sources of supply, the costs of taking action as a voter, which are, as I have hinted, considerable, are compounded by the difficulty of acquiring the information from government on which this action is based. Voters are faced with an "adverse selection" problem for the sole source of information on the costs of the demanded service will be the government administration. Given the further problem of identifying output measures for government services, the opportunities, as in monopolistic firms, for X-inefficiency are considerable. While this line of explanation suggests that government services are likely to be more costly than they need be, it does not indicate how opportunities for X-inefficiency are translated into a faster relative rate of growth in government expenditure.

Two "back-up" hypotheses have been used to buttress the influence of supply factors. The first is the contention that productivity gains are less likely to be reaped in government-type products and services than in the private economy generally. This is because such products and services are inherently labour-intensive. Therefore, if wage rates in the public sector rise at broadly the same rate as in the private sector, no increases (or relatively slower increases) in productivity in the former sector will result in a faster rate of growth of expenditure than in the latter sector. Clearly, this "change in the terms of trade" argument rests on the important assumption that the income elasticity of demand for government services in real terms is equal to or greater than unity. In short, it accepts that "demand propulsion" is a necessary condition for the Baumol effect[1] to work. The second

1. For the original exposition of this effect as applied to the public sector, see WILLIAM J. BAUMOL and WALLACE J. OATES, *The Theory of Environmental Policy: Ex-*

contention is that, to some extent at least, supply will increase its own demand after a point where G/GDP is, say, over 20 per cent. This is because a vested interest is created in government in the form of those whom it employs. Not only do government employees have opportunities for "rigging" the terms of trade, but, as they grow in number, they have added voting strength.

With this last factor before us, the analogy with the growth of a company or an industry seems to have been pushed far beyond reasonable limits. However, summing up our conspectus, the value of looking at the growth of the government as an interaction of supply and demand factors is that it stresses that the various identified influences on government growth may be complements rather than rivals. Just as Marshall resolved the debate about the relative importance of demand and supply in determining price and output with his "scissors" analogy, it seems sensible to expect that the explanatory power of different theories, while they may vary from one decade to another, may retain some such power at the same time. One concludes from this that, having entered the era of empirical testing of such theories on a grand scale, such a view would seem to point towards the simultaneous testing of demand-dominated and supply-dominated in one econometric model. However, it would be wholly out of tune with what has been said so far to postulate a model in which some equilibrium between supply and demand is automatically reached. As Lybeck[1] has argued if "demand exceeds supply" it is reasonable to suppose that politicians aided by bureaucrats will adjust supply to demand, which will fit their interests, and will be made possible by the ability of governments to run deficits. Likewise, if "supply exceeds demand", *ex-ante*, then it is also reasonable to suppose that the politicians,

ternalities, Public Outlays and the Quality of Life, Englewood Cliffs, N. J.: Prentice-Hall, 1975. For an exposition and critique of the 'Baumol effect' see ALAN T. PEACOCK, 'The Problem of Public Expenditure Growth in Post-Industrial Society', in Bo GUSTAFSSON, ed., *Post-Industrial Society*, London: Croom Helm, 1978, pp. 80-95, reprinted in PEACOCK, *The Economic Analysis of Government and Related Themes, op. cit.*, pp. 105-17.

1. See JOHAN A. LYBECK, *The Growth of Government in Developed Economies, op. cit.*, p. 91.

as actual decision makers, will be able to effect the necessary adjustment of demand.

It would take me too far away from my main theme to review the evolution of empirical testing procedures,[1] for my purpose is to consider in more detail than I have done so far the importance of "historical input" into the analysis of public sector growth. However, some words of warning are necessary about the scope and method of testing procedures.

Firstly, the quality of data for individual countries is good and comparable indicators of government growth can be identified, but only for the last 25 years or so. If interest centres in relatively short-run situations, this presents no difficulty and at least a case could be made for saying that 25 years is enough to identify causes of government sector growth which have some bearing on how growth might be controlled in the foreseeable future.

Secondly, testing models assume fixed elasticity coefficients relating the determinants of growth (e.g. population change, growth in *GDP* etc.) and *G*. However convenient this may be for testing purposes, it assumes relatively smooth changes through time. There are no "structural breaks", as represented by wars (leading to alterations in frontiers, major changes in income and wealth distribution etc.) and revolutions. The longer the period of time under consideration, the less plausible the assumption that the equations contain all the relevant variables and that the coefficients can plausibly be regarded as constants. The combination of lower quality of data for years before World War II and the problem of incorporating structural breaks make it understandable if the study of the longer-term is now somewhat out of fashion in an age when no hypothesis appears to deserve the name unless it is capable of being tested![2]

1. For an excellent survey see JOHAN A. LYBECK and MAGNUS HENREKSON, eds., *Explaining the Growth of Government*, Amsterdam: North Holland, 1988, Chapter 1, pp. 3-19.

2. For further discussion of the problems of economic testing see the perceptive critique of JACK WISEMAN, 'The Political Economy of Government Revenues', in ALDO CHIANCONE and KEN MESSERE, eds., *Changes in Revenue Structure*, Detroit, Mi.: Wayne State University Press, 1989. He particularly stresses the difficulties encountered in using empirical analysis in order to rank explanations of public sector growth.

3. The Past as Prologue

Let me return now to my thesis about the demand for historical perspective. In this lecture I shall adopt a very strict selection process and choose an example from the history of ideas which has had actual influence. It would equally well illustrate my thesis if I could pick examples of "neglected theories" which "deserve" resurrection, but I do not want to involve myself in forecasting whether any such objects of neglect, as a result of exhumation, are likely to inspire future writing on the theory of public sector growth. I have already indicated my choice of de Tocqueville.

A little historical background may be useful. As all Italian scholars must be aware, one of the great political debates of the nineteenth century concerned the consequences of introducing a universal franchise. Confining our attention to the economists,[1] the question of most interest to the Classicists was the relation between the extension of the franchise and the securing of the operations of free market principles. They faced a dilemma for, on the one hand, the concept of economic freedom seemed to suggest political freedom as its necessary complement, whereas, on the other hand, there was no guarantee that political freedom, secured through extending the franchise, would guarantee votes for free market principles. The resolution of the dilemma appeared to lie in extending the franchise only so far as it was compatible with the disposition of individuals to accept the sanctity of private property. In the longer run, if free market principles were allowed to operate, the distribution of property would become more widely dispersed, and as its virtues became more widely appreciated so could the franchise be widened until Universal (male !) adult (for James Mill[2] those of forty years or

1. The issue of the place of the franchise in economic thinking is discussed in detail in a highly original essay by T. Hutchison. My own account has been influenced by his approach. See TERENCE W. HUTCHISON, *The Politics and Philosophy of Economics: Marxians, Keynesians and Austrians*, Oxford: Blackwell, 1981, Chapter 2.

2. I would not like anyone to gain the impression that I am mocking Mill *père*. He pioneered the invocation of the principle of utility as a justification for representative government. See JAMES MILL, *An Essay on Government* (1819); with an Introduction by ERNEST BARKER, Cambridge: Cambridge University Press, 1937.

more!) suffrage might be attained. I pass over some of the pre-liminary skirmishes which the Classical economists had with their principles of freedom and draw your attention to a re-markable posthumous article which Ricardo's friends published in the *Scotsman* in 1824. Ricardo first of all states his principle: "So essential does it appear to me, to the cause of good govern-ment, that the rights of property should be held sacred, that I would agree to deprive those of the elective franchise against whom it could be alleged that they considered it their interest to invade them."

He then considers how this constrains the width of the franchise, concluding that

... in fact it can be only amongst the most needy in the community that such an opinion can be entertained.

Next he interpolates his concern about the consequences of a universal franchise, namely that of the temptation it gives to support equalisation of fortunes but

[the] man of small fortune must know how little he would obtain by such a division could be no adequate compensation for the over-turning of a principle which renders the produce of his industry secure.

Finally, he offers his policy conclusion:

I am convinced that an extension of the suffrage, far short of making it universal, will substantially secure to the people the good govern-ment they wish for, and therefore I deprecate the demand for the universality of the elective franchise – at the same time, I feel con-fident that the effects of the measure which would satisfy me would have so beneficial an effect on the public mind, would be the means of so rapidly increasing the knowledge and intelligence of the public, that, in a limited space of time after this first measure of reform were granted, we might, with the utmost safety, extend the right of voting for members of Parliament to every class of the people.[1]

---

1. DAVID RICARDO, *Works and Correspondence*, edited by PIERO SRAFFA with the collaboration of MAURICE H. DOBB, vol. v, *Speeches and Evidence*, Cambridge: Cambridge University Press, 1962, pp. 495-503.

Ricardo, therefore, takes a somewhat optimistic view of the progress towards the universal franchise. It was one which political writers of the perspicacity of de Tocqueville, and, let it be said, Marx, were to question in the light of French experience leading up to the 1848 revolution.[1] However, de Tocqueville's reputation amongst his contemporaries, as a thinker rather than as the prominent politician he became, rested on his close observation of what actually appeared to happen in a country, the United States of America, in which it was generally held that universal suffrage had actually arrived, though we would certainly demur at the implied definition of universality, given the presence of slavery in that country.

De Tocqueville's analysis comes in a remarkable chapter of his *Democracy in America*[2] which all concerned with public economics should read. He implicitly accepts and elaborates very considerably on the Classical economists' contention that the universal franchise creates a demand for redistribution. Thus de Tocqueville:

Let us . . . suppose that the legislative authority is vested in the lowest orders: there are two striking reasons which show that the tendency of the expenditure be to increase rather than to diminish. As the great majority of those who create the laws are possessed of no property upon which taxes can be imposed, all the money which is spent for the community appears to be spent to their advantage, at no cost of their own; and those who are possessed of some little property readily find means of regulating the taxes so that they are burdensome to the wealthy and profitable to the poor, although the rich are unable to take the same advantage when they are in possession of Government

and later

the government of the democracy is the only one under which the power which lays on taxes escapes the payment of them.[3]

1. See, J. P. MAYER, 'Preface' to ALEXIS DE TOCQUEVILLE, *Recollections*, edited by J. P. MAYER and A. P. KERR, New York: Doubleday 1971.
2. ALEXIS DE TOCQUEVILLE, *Democracy in America*, Oxford: Oxford University Press, 1965. The original, *De la Démocratie en Amérique*, appeared in two parts, the first in 1835 and the second in 1840. The translation of each part by Henry Reeve appeared in each case in the year of publication in the original French.
3. *Ibid.*, p. 150.

This "demand for redistribution", as we call it today, is further elaborated by de Tocqueville and is not simply reflected in a tax system which exempts the poor. It also takes the form of public "improvements" for which

in democracies, where the rules labour under privations, they can only be courted by such means as improve their well-being and these improvements cannot take place without a sacrifice of money. When a people begins to reflect upon its situation, it discovers a multitude of wants to which it had not before been subject, and to satisfy these exigencies recourse must be had to the coffers of the State.[1]

At this juncture, one might well ask whether this learning process does any more than increase G, without necessarily increasing G/GDP. De Tocqueville comes as near to saying that he is talking about G/GDP when he adds: "Hence it arises that the public charges increase in proportion as civilization spreads, and that imposts are augmented as knowledge pervades the community."[2]

Thus the knowledge of what government action can achieve on behalf of the majority engenders a taste for publicly-provided services, but might there not be economies of scale in their provision? De Tocqueville does not consider the influence of scale on costs, but he claims that "democracy . . . does not understand the art of being economical".[3] This claim is not based on the standard argument that X-inefficiency abounds in the delivery of government services. Indeed, he observes that the envy of the majority who are relatively poor promotes strong resistance to the payment of salaries to the executive ranks of public officials above those of the common people. The growth in public expenditure is propelled by the rapid changes in taste resulting from competition between governments in power for a limited length of time:

As the designs which [democracy] entertains are frequently changed and the agents of those designs are still more frequently removed, its undertakings are often ill conducted or left unfinished: in the former

1. *Ibid.*, p. 153.
2. *Ibid.*, p. 153.
3. *Ibid.*, p. 153.

45

case the State spends sums out of all proportion to the end which it proposes to accomplish; in the second, the expenses itself is unprofitable.[1]

So far, de Tocqueville's argument presages that of the modern hypotheses of public sector growth which we have already reviewed, but he adds the original twist which has appealed to modern writers. Ricardo, we noticed, observed that provided one "goes easy", there was nothing to fear from the ultimate extension of the franchise. De Tocqueville buttressed this argument in an original way:

... the extravagance of democracy is, however, less to be dreaded in proportion as the people acquire a share of property, because on the one hand the contributions of the rich are then less needed, and, on the other, it is more difficult to lay on taxes which do not affect the interests of the lower classes. On this account universal suffrage would be less dangerous in France than in England, because in the latter country the property on which taxes may be levied is in fewer hands. America, where the great majority of the citizens possess some fortune, is in a still more favourable position than France.[2]

A few years ago[3] I reproduced de Tocqueville's argument in diagrammatic form in which the growth of G/GDP is positive function of (i) the extension of the franchise; and (ii) the inequality of income distribution. We assumed, like de Tocqueville, that the decision rule for introduction of government measures will be simple majority rule. All voters maximise their utility by maximising their income, after taking account of taxes and both money and real transfers from government. The decisive voter is the median voter and voters are partitioned into those with incomes below the median level who choose candidates for the legislature who favour redistribution, whereas voters with incomes above the median level prefer lower taxes and less redistribution. Historically the spread of the franchise increased

1. *Ibid.*, p. 153.
2. *Ibid.*, p. 152.
3. ALAN T. PEACOCK, 'Reducing Government Expenditure Growth: A British View', in HERBERT GIERSCH, ed., *Reassessing the Role of Government in the Mixed Economy*, Tübingen: Mohr (Paul Siebeck), 1983, pp. 1-24.

the proportion of voters with relatively low income. The distribution of income of voters becomes more unequal and so the median income voter's position moves down the income distribution scale, raising the number of voters in favour of redistribution (see Figure 2).

The rectangle *abdfh* represents the initial "equilibrium" position. Starting at point *a*, where the franchise covers, say, 30 per cent of the adult population, the given income distribution identifies a given percentage of voters, denoted by *oc*, with incomes below the average. The combination of the extent of the

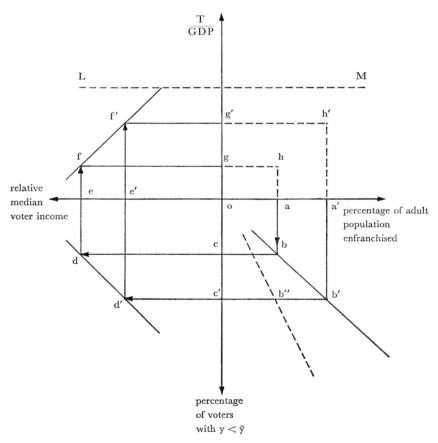

Figure 2. De Tocqueville's Cross

47

franchise and the given distribution of income, identifies the appropriate median voter income oe, the median voter position being crucial for the determination of T/GDP which is represented by the distance og (all axes are positive, of course).

Consider what happens when the franchise is extended. The percentage of adult population enfranchised moves, say, to oa', and the percentage of voters with $y > \bar{y}$ will increase, with the enfranchisement of poorer voters from, say, oc to oc'. It may be noted that the same effect would be achieved if the franchise were not extended but the distribution of income became more unequal in the sense described. The relative median voter income would fall, and the decisive vote would shift the T/GDP ratio upwards. The final result is shown in the rectangle $a'b'd'f'h'$. It is not possible in this four-quadrant system to show explicitly the effect of T/GDP on G/GDP, and the possibility that there is a limit to the growth in T/GDP is crudely represented by the upper bound LM. Nor is close investigation made of the shape as well as the slope of the various curves, which need not be linear.

4. The Stimulus to Present Thinking

De Tocqueville's approach is an example of "grand design" speculation which stops us in our tracks and makes us reappraise our approach to a problem, a present-day example close to our subject being Mancur Olson's *Rise and Decline of Nations*.[1] When it comes to the practical problems of considering the consequences of public expenditure growth and what might be done, if anything, about that growth, it is unlikely to be more than a point of departure. However, before dismissing his approach solely as a stimulus to those who have developed his ideas, there are some features of it on which further comment seems required.

First, to isolate only one section of de Tocqueville's predictions about the progress of democracy is to distort his purpose as well as to underestimate other features of his study which have bearing on the growth of the public sector. To consider only the latter point, de Tocqueville offers the insight that the promotion of the interests of those to whom the franchise is a new-found power demands the centralisation of government, for only in this way can the power of the aristocracy, based on its feudal and therefore regional hegemony, be broken. One reason, he claims, why centralisation was not likely to proceed so fast and so far in the United States was the absence of an aristocracy with entrenched privileges.

Second, his "grand design" theory, like many of his general speculations, is firmly based on observation of human behaviour. His predictions of the evolution of democracies do not have recourse to mysterious impersonal forces which impel progress along predestinate paths. As he remarks in his closing paragraph of *Democracy in America*:

I am aware that many of my contemporaries maintain that nations are never their own masters here below, and that they necessarily obey some insurmountable and unintelligent power, arising from anterior events, from their race, or from the soil and climate of their

1. See MANCUR OLSON, *The Rise and Decline of Nations: Economic Growth, Stagnation, and Social Rigidities*, New Haven, Ct.: Yale University Press, 1982, especially Chapter 7.

49

country. Such principles are false and cowardly; such principles can never produce aught but feeble men and pusillanimous nations. Providence has not created mankind entirely independent or entirely free. It is true that around every man a fatal circle is traced, beyond which he cannot pass; but within the wide verge of that circle he is powerful and free: as it is with man, so with communities.[1]

The lines of enquiry suggested by de Tocqueville's analysis are many, but our concern here is with those of his speculations which have influenced recent discussion.[2] Probably the most interesting idea emanating from his "demand for redistribution" argument is that it suggests reasons for limitations on the growth in G/GDP which are derived from electoral behaviour reflecting the self-interest of voters.

It could be that redistribution could continue if economic growth is associated with rising inequality of incomes, as Simon Kuznets once suggested. However, if taxpayers/voters can choose between consumption and leisure, then the reduction in the price of leisure resulting from the rising tax burden on the upper income voters may lower the growth in taxable income and put a brake on the growth in the size of government. Assuming a balanced budget, then the proportion of the tax "take" to GDP would remain roughly constant and so would the proportion of government spending on goods and services and transfers as a proportion of GDP.

This argument becomes much more complicated if one extends what de Tocqueville called the "verge of the circle" constraining the individual voter's position as a decision maker, in order to consider the individual's perception of his future position in the income scale. A voter now in the lowest income quartile

1. DE TOCQUEVILLE, *Democracy in America*, *op. cit.*, pp. 598-99.
2. It is noteworthy that the 'demand for redistribution' has been regarded by contemporary Italian writers as a major influence on government expenditure growth, though the models tested are not confined to vertical redistribution. See ILDE RIZZO, 'Regional Disparities and Decentralization as Determinants of Public Sector Expenditure Growth in Italy (1960-81)', in FORTE and PEACOCK, eds., *Public Expenditure and Government Growth*, *op. cit.*, pp. 65-82; GIORGIO BROSIO and CARLA MARCHESE, 'The Growth of Public Expenditure in Italy since the Second World War', in LYBECK and HENREKSON, eds., *Explaining the Growth of Government*, *op. cit.*, pp. 187-200.

might have expectations of moving up the income scale as he gains in skill and experience. Trading off present post-tax income against future post-tax income may indicate to him that the discounted value of his income aggregated through time would be higher if he did not vote in favour of taxing the relatively rich. However, a voter who is at present in an income bracket well above the median income level may be in favour of state transfers in the form of social security payments as an insurance against uncertain income prospects in the future. In short, maximising income through time under conditions of uncertainty with attitudes to risk which are not distributed according to present income levels suggest that the identification of the median voter with the median income receiver is very much an over-simplification. A possible defence of de Tocqueville's position is that in his day not only was the income distribution highly skewed in France and England, but the poor lived at levels of subsistence and in precarious conditions where expectations of moving up the income scale were severely limited and very high rates of discount would be applied to future income.

The prospect of a limit to the growth in G/GDP seems dimmed further by the opportunities given to governments to overcome the limitations on raising T/GDP by substituting an increase in the rate of borrowing. If we stick to the spirit, if not to the letter, of de Tocqueville's analysis, then we must relate the use of his fiscal weapon to demand (i.e. voter) pressure. This needs to be said because the use of borrowing rather than taxation as a means of promoting the growth in government expenditure is normally associated with attempts by politicians and public servants to exploit "fiscal illusion". Thus Buchanan and Wagner have argued that an increase in government borrowing in order to finance an increase in government expenditure creates the illusion of a fall in the price of government services relative to private goods and services.[1] De Tocqueville does not specifically consider how his demand for redistribution would be affected by voter consent to increased borrowing but the explanation

1. JAMES M. BUCHANAN and RICHARD E. WAGNER, *Democracy in Deficit: The Political Legacy of Lord Keynes*, London: Academic Press, 1977.

of the growth in government borrowing in the latter half of the twentieth century in industrial countries could be explained, in part at least, in terms of a voting model. Present generation voters may perceive borrowing as a method by which they are able to exploit future generations, who are *ipso facto* disenfranchised, and who will be bequeathed with the duty of repayment. However, this is to assume that voters are subject to another kind of illusion, namely that no costs are imposed upon them. If the proportion of G financed by borrowing increases and if governments issue interest-bearing debt to the private sector, then interest payments to present generations of taxpayers/voters may make the pre-tax distribution of income more unequal and at the same time may encourage the relatively rich to substitute investment income for labour income. The translation of these complicated distributional and incentive effects into a demand for G becomes much more complicated. Correspondingly, if taxpayers/voters require that governments cover revenue deficits by money creation there is a prospect that this will increase the rate of inflation. The interests of taxpayers/voters at any given initial position in the income distribution, before inflation accelerates, may be very diverse and not identical, as the model implies. Identifying the median voter again becomes difficult and the desire to shift the burden of current redistribution through the budget onto future generations may not be so clearly discerned. That being so, to associate the growth of public debt as a financing mechanism for government expenditure purely with voter demand is questionable, and one is forced back, perhaps, into considering more closely the Buchanan/Wagner-type thesis.

My own view is that the intergeneration "bargaining problem", as it might be termed, is more forcibly illustrated by the ability of present generations of voters to award themselves future claims on government expenditure through the incurring of unfunded obligations, a point to which brief reference has already been made in Section 2 above. The most striking example of such government expenditure is represented by state retirement schemes, whereby the present generation of voters who are members of the working population vote themselves retirement benefits which represent claims on future consumption which will have to be foregone by future generations of workers who have no say in the initial decision. Trying to pre-empt the inter-generation distribution of income in this way also has its counter-part in the favourable tax treatment of retirement incomes and all kinds of price reductions (such as subsidised rail and road travel) from which retired persons can benefit. There is therefore a strong temptation for governments to stipulate future benefits for present generations without requiring that these benefits be "paid for" wholly from a levy, such as a social security tax, on present generations, which would establish property rights in future benefits. Of course, the unenfranchised future generations, when faced with a pre-emptive strike on the income distribution made by the (now) retired population, may not necessarily con-sider that they should honour a bargain in which they had no say. But now we are in deep water, for it is not necessary to suppose that intergeneration contracts, even if one-sided, can be summed up in the form of what appears to be a zero-sum game. For example, present generation voters, to a varying extent, will include the welfare of their children in their utility function, and this will clearly modify voter behaviour designed to reflect the interests of present generations in their claim to resources in the future.[1] I am content here merely to illustrate once again the extensive lines of enquiry stimulated by de Tocqueville's analysis.

---

1. For further discussion on these issues, see ALAN T. PEACOCK, 'Is there a Public Debt Problem in Developed Countries?', in BERNARD P. HERBER, ed., *Public Finance and Public Debt*, Detroit, Mi.: Wayne State University Press, 1986, pp. 29-41.

5. Summary and Conclusions

I have argued that the search for some all embracing economic theory of public expenditure growth is now generally recognised as a chimera. This must be so, as the analogy with a dynamic theory of supply and demand would indicate. We can categorise what are likely to be the main influences on that growth; we can formulate "empirical laws" such as Wagner's Law or "Baumol's Law" which can serve as points of departure for detailed analysis of particular aspects of that growth. In the last analysis, de Tocqueville has put his finger on the most important feature of trying to explain what is happening or is likely to happen to the growth of the public sector. That growth depends on the resolution of forces which are governed by human action and testable models must therefore embody a clear delineation of the participants in political decisions and what motivates them. Schumpeter, in his characteristic magisterial style, summed up the achievement of *Democracy in America* in the following words:

What is the nature of the performance that produced one of the "great books" of the period? It conveyed no discovery of fact or principle; it did not use any elaborate technique; it did nothing to court the public (especially the American public). An extremely intelligent mind, nurtured on the fruits of an old civilisation took infinite trouble as to observations and brilliantly subdued them to serve an analytic purpose. This was all. But it is much. And I know of no other book that would train us better in the art of succeeding in this particular kind of political analysis.[1]

I think I have made a good *prima facie* case for my general thesis about the contribution of historical perspective to a central issue in public choice analysis. It is a sobering thought, nevertheless, that Schumpeter, so far as I know, is the only major historian of economic thought who even hints that de Tocqueville has anything to teach us, and he does not do much more

---

1. JOSEPH A. SCHUMPETER, *History of Economic Analysis*, edited by ELIZABETH BOODY SCHUMPETER, New York: Oxford University Press, 1954, p. 433.

than sing his praises. My own discovery of de Tocqueville's contribution was a pure accident and I might have completely overlooked it had I not developed a close interest in public sector growth. It is also an interesting coincidence that this contribution was simultaneously rediscovered by two colleagues, Meltzer and Richard, who have done so much to elaborate his basic propositions and to test them.[1] I cannot be sure that my interest in the evolution of economic ideas concerning public sector growth is a good example to follow, or that there are other thinkers in Schumpeter's "lumber room" that deserve the same attention. However, I hope that judgment can be deferred until consideration is given to the other aspects of my main theme to which the next lectures are devoted.

1. See ALAN H. MELTZER and SCOTT F. RICHARD, 'Tests of a Rational Theory of the Size of Government', *Public Choice*, vol. 41, No. 3, 1983, pp. 403-18.

THIRD LECTURE
The Economic Consequences of Public Sector Growth

1. Introduction. – 2. The Constituents of the Bureaucratic Model. – 3. The Classical View of Bureaucracy. – 4. Bureaucracy with a Classical Utility Function. – 5. The Infection of Inefficiency.

1. Introduction

The theory of public choice is characterised by a distinct view of the development of society, as it is applied to public sector growth, namely that individuals, acting alone or in combination, are rational self-interested decision-makers, which does not necessarily mean that they are not mindful of the interests of others. As we shall observe, the view taken of human nature by the Classical economists, notably Hume and Smith, who have influenced but have not always been fully understood by public choice theorists, is one of considerable subtlety.[1]

The public-choice view of human action not only provides us with an agenda for the study of the determinants of public sector growth. It does so also for the study of the consequences of that growth. Broadly speaking, the growth which reflects human choices reinforces the tendency for individual voters/taxpayers to form interest groups in order to use the state as a means of capturing benefits, normally at the expense of other groups. Unless powerful interest groups are able to reach agreement on bargaining rules which restrict their freedom, "group sclerosis"[2] may result, which will be reflected in economic stagnation. This is because concern for immediate group interests

---

1. For support to this view, see RICHARD A. MUSGRAVE, 'Leviathan Cometh – Or Does He?', in HELEN F. LADD and NICOLAUS TIDEMAN, eds., *Tax and Expenditure Limitations*, Washington, D.C.: The Urban Institute, 1981, reprinted in RICHARD A. MUSGRAVE, *Public Finance in a Democratic Society*, vol. II, Brighton: Wheatsheaf, 1986, p. 227, footnote 11.

2. Following the analysis developed by MANCUR OLSON in *The Rise and Decline of Nations, op. cit.*, especially Chapter 2.

directs effort towards using the state as a redistributive mechanism rather than towards improving economic performance. The "invisible hand" loses its power as the "system of natural liberty" is destroyed; the pursuit of self-interest through interest groupings does not promote but acts against the interests of all (or most).

It would be wrong, however, to give the impression that the power of government is completely emasculated as the public sector grows. Public choice theory has latterly laid particular stress on the fact that the redistributive battle is not reflected simply in transfers of income effected by fiscal action. It is also reflected in a combination of both public *financing* of redistributive gains (and losses) and public *provision* of services directed towards the benefit of particular interest groups, notably education, health and environmental services. The growth of such services has resulted in a growth in the relative size of non-marketed output coupled with a growing proportion of the working population whose economic fortunes are not directly determined solely by market forces. The very pursuit of interests associated with private sector groups generates another set of interests associated with those who supply public services. It is this set of interests, usually labelled "the bureaucracy", with which this lecture is concerned, and with the instructive contribution of the Classical economists to the modern discussion of the consequences of the growth of bureaucracy.

In analysing the consequences of this growth, as measured, say, by the growth in the relative size of public employment, I shall take a restricted view of "the consequences". I shall follow the precedent of recent discussion which has focused on the alleged "economic inefficiencies" associated with the motivation and power of bureaucrats, and the associated loss of "consumer sovereignty". The reader needs to be reminded, perhaps, that this approach would hardly satisfy those who would be concerned with the broader consequences of public sector growth or who would argue that, in considering "economic" consequences, one should look beyond individual consumer sovereignty to a judgement of these consequences based on some "social welfare function" containing other arguments such as distributional, stabilisation and growth criteria.

I think it would be useful to look briefly at these alternative approaches, if only to bring out more clearly the distinctive features of the public choice approach and particularly the very different view taken about the interface between the citizen and the state.

A much broader view of the consequences of the growth of government is taken, of course, by a writer no doubt sympathetic to the libertarian bias commonly found amongst public choice theorists, namely Hayek.[1] The message of *The Road to Serfdom* is clear and simple. Society risks the complete subjugation of citizens to the arbitrary power of the state as government grows. This has happened when governments are "captured" by intellectual ideas of socialists which maintain that "the good society" requires massive state intervention. The only remedy is to fight against these intellectual errors which hold society in thrall. Of course, Hayek envisages a state using a whole range of planning instruments extending far beyond the fiscal system, but he and many of his followers have criticised "liberal socialists" who support a mixed economy on the grounds that it is an illusion to suppose that if G/GDP is large the economy can maintain any vestiges of a competitive free market system which is an essential element in the preservation of freedom.[2]

It would take us too far away from the central theme if we proceeded to analyse the steps in Hayek's argument. The important thing to notice is that it implicitly assumes that the bulk of humanity will act entirely passively when ideological statements are translated into policy action. If individuals maximise, it will be subject to the constraints imposed on them by government so that, as government grows, the constraints become more and more binding.

As I am concerned with historical perspective, I cannot avoid

1. FRIEDRICH A. VON HAYEK, *The Road to Serfdom*, London: Routledge and Kegan Paul, 1944. See also *Hayek's 'Serfdom' Revisited. Essays by Economists, Philosophers and Political Scientists on 'The Road to Serfdom' after 40 Years*, London: Institute of Economic Affairs, 1984, for a number of perceptive essays celebrating the 40th anniversary of the appearance of Hayek's famous work.

2. See S. C. LITTLECHILD, *The Fallacy of the Mixed Economy: An 'Austrian' Critique of Economic Thinking and Policy*, Second edition, London: Institute of Economic Affairs, 1968.

the temptation of reminding you that the views of Hayek and some of his followers, such as Rothbard,[1] who have taken an even more extreme position about the passivity of the masses, are anticipated by our old friend Alexis de Tocqueville. Towards the end of his classic work he writes on the consequences of the growth of centralised governmental power as follows:

The will of man is not shattered but softened, bent and guided; men are seldom forced by it to act, but they are constantly restrained from acting. Such a power does not destroy, but it prevents existence, it does not tyrannize, but it compresses, enervates, extinguishes, and stupefies a people, till each nation is reduced to be nothing better than a flock of timid and industrious animals of which government is the shepherd. I have always thought that servitude of the regular, quiet and gentle kind which I have just described might be combined more easily than is commonly believed with some of the outward forms of freedom, and that it might even establish itself under the wing of the sovereignty of the people.[2]

This is a position far removed from the idea that interests are what determine how the world is ruled. It is an example of what Norman Barry in a splendid essay has called "the Keynesian cliché".[3] Keynes implicitly rejects public choice when, in a famous phrase, he says "soon or late it is ideas not vested interests which are dangerous for good or evil". It is revealing that Hayek subscribes to much the same view. Certainly, one might argue, if anyone has a vested interest in such a view it must be intellectuals, and this may be a major reason why it had such a powerful hold on the imagination of economists and other observers concerned with the broader aspects of economic development!

  The alternative "broad" approach is also of interest because of its view of motivation of those (all of us nowadays) affected by the pursuit of economic policies which generally assume a

  1. See MURRAY N. ROTHBARD, *The Ethics of Liberty*, Atlantic Highlands, N. J.: Humanities Press, 1982.
  2. Quoted by HANNES H. GISSURARSON, 'The Only Truly Progressive Policy . . .', in *Hayek's 'Serfdom' Revisited, op. cit.*, p. 19.
  3. NORMAN BARRY, 'Ideas versus Interests: The Classical Liberal Dilemma', in *Hayek's 'Serfdom' Revisited, op. cit.*, pp. 43-64.

relatively large public sector. It would take us far outside the immediate concern of this lecture to consider the conventional theory of economic policy on which it is based,[1] which assumes that it is both desirable and possible for the governments of large industrial nations simultaneously to pursue growth, distributional and stabilisation objectives. It simplifies my task if I concentrate on "economic performance", as measured by *GNP* per capita, which in any case is the indicator singled out by those international agencies such as the Organization for Economic Co-operation and Development which monitor this performance on behalf of such nations. In fact, a recent OECD Report[2] offers a most useful distillation of recent economic thinking coloured by this approach. Economic performance, it is argued, is adversely affected by a large and growing public sector and this implies that "welfare" is lower than it might otherwise be. The welfare costs are imposed by the financing of the growth in the public sector. Thus, although the magnitude of the effects may be a matter for dispute, deficit financing can produce adverse effects on investment through "crowding out" of private investment in the short run and by the servicing costs in the long run which raise taxes. Current methods of raising taxes, conditioned to some extent by distributional considerations, increase the marginal welfare costs to taxpayers and reduce the incentive to work, though again the appropriate methodology and the magnitude of the observed effects may not be fully agreed.[3] The conclusion is reached that

... in recent years, evidence has begun to accumulate that the economic costs of financing government spending are not as small as was once thought, a finding that is particularly strong at the margin: the costs of increasing the size of the public sector, as well as the

1. For a useful critique of this theory, see PAUL MOSLEY, *The Making of Economic Policy: Theory and Evidence from Britain and the United States since 1945*, Brighton: Wheatsheaf, 1984, Chapter 1.

2. *Structural Adjustment and Economic Performance*, Paris: Organization for Economic Co-operation and Development, 1987, particularly Chapter 10.

3. For a recent methodological survey, see E. K. BROWNING, 'On the Marginal Welfare Cost of Taxation', *American Economic Review*, March 1987, pp. 11-23.

gains from reducing it, are significantly larger than the average econ-omic cost of public sector spending.[1]

Although "perceptions" (which means perceptions of policy-makers) may differ about the trade-offs between the objective of economic performance and others, such as equity, it is gener-ally advocated that the policy solution to the costs of public sector growth lies in reforming the tax system by moving to-wards consumption-based and away from income-based taxes.

What is striking in this statement is that the perception of the taxpayer as a passive adjuster reacting to various stimuli under the control of the public authorities is common to both these approaches. In the Hayekian model, the individual is "deluded" into accepting large government by the false attraction of ideas or by fear of those in power who have absorbed such ideas. In the "economic policy" model, his reactions to the policy measures of the public authorities are summed up solely in effects on incentives to work, save and invest, subject to fiscal constraints. The taxpayer/voter has no direct say in the formu-lation of the welfare function and cannot de-stabilise it through political action. Furthermore, in the particular analysis under scrutiny, no mention is made of the possible effect of the growth of the public sector on the creation of market imperfections and on the growth in the resource inputs employed in non-marketed activities. In consequence, the possibility of increasing economic inefficiency within the public sector is ignored.

In the analysis which follows, the public servant is viewed neither as a potential instrument for the suppression of the rights of others nor as the farsighted dispassionate controller of our economic destiny. Like the members of other interest groups, their actions may be circumscribed by the actions of other interest groups, but they too have "instruments of political participation" which make it possible for them to negotiate with other groups rather than to require them to act as passive adjusters to the actions of others.

---

1. *Structural Adjustment and Economic Performance, op. cit.*, p. 364.

2. The Constituents of the Bureaucratic Model

The *loci classici* of the modern economic theory of bureaucracy are the works by Niskanen[1] and Tullock.[2] I shall present a formalised version of their original model and then subject it to a criticism which adopts what may be termed a "Classical perspective". We reverse the usual process found in the study of the history of ideas, and derive our criticisms of present day modelling from the writings on similar matters by Hume, Smith, and others.

The bureaucratic paradigm follows closely the methodology of the economics of the "individual firm":

(i) The bureau is in the charge of a "manager", a government official of appropriate seniority, who is assumed to maximise his/her utility. However, unlike the individual entrepreneur in the market economy, he/she cannot appropriate any net profits over and above the costs of producing any given level of output. The manager has to maximise his utility by other means. The arguments in his utility function reflect such positive influences as the prestige of controlling a large staff, the consolations derived from the perquisites of office (subject to any constraints placed on salary and expense claims by the Ministry of Finance) and the minimisation of the "hassle" of his position by his skill and reputation in managing his staff. Niskanen[3] provides an ingenious solution for reducing these motives to a measurable quantity. Ignoring the ease of managing the bureau, all the arguments point in one direction – towards the maximisation of the budget under the control of the manager of the bureau;

(ii) The government bureau is the sole supplier of the product. Two interesting problems of definition are raised by this kind

1. WILLIAM A. NISKANEN, *Bureaucracy and Representative Government*, Chicago, Ill.: Aldine, 1971. For an admirable exposition and critique of the Niskanen position, alongside close study of the economist's approach to the study of bureaucratic organisation, see the comprehensive survey by PETER M. JACKSON, *The Political Economy of Bureaucracy*, Deddington, Oxford: Philip Allan, 1982, Chapters 5 and 6.
2. GORDON TULLOCK, *The Politics of Bureaucracy*, Washington, D.C.: Public Affairs Press, 1965.
3. NISKANEN, *Bureaucracy and Representative Government*, *op. cit.*, p. 22.

of statement. The first is common to both public and private monopoly. It is a well known fallacy to suppose that the sole seller of a separately identifiable product or service necessarily has monopoly power, for monopoly power can only be defined in terms of market power, i.e. sensitivity of the quantity demanded to a change in price. In the private sector, the demand for tickets for the sole producer of, say, Shakespeare plays, is a function of their price relative to other sources of entertainment, including not only the plays, say, of Pirandello, but also the other ways of spending a pleasant cultural evening. Likewise even a government service usually regarded as a monopoly, such as defence, may be a substitute for other services which are designed to produce the same end. If the ultimate aim is "deterrence", then investment in diplomatic skills may offer a competing substitute. Whether purchasers of government services think in these terms is an open question, but it is at least conceivable that there can be some competition between bureaux, unless they have the incentive and the opportunity to collude against the purchaser. The second problem is particular to the public sector. How does one define and measure the output of services which are not sold in the market? The search for an answer reveals how careful one must be in assessing the efficiency of government services. A familiar example comes from police services. Should the measure of output be the number of criminals caught (perhaps weighted by the enormity of their offences!), or the reduction in the number of crimes committed? Our analysis has to assume that there is some measurable form of output;

(iii) The purchasers of the bureau's "output", say the government in power, will demand more of the output, the lower is its "price". This statement seems a very doubtful one when services are not in fact priced and the definition of "output" is obscure − how can one draw a demand curve? A government or sponsoring agent appointed by government to demand the service in question must have *some* conception of the units of output and also some evaluation of the service provided. For *any given level of budget* it is reasonable to suppose that the purchaser will prefer a perceived higher output to a lower one. It may therefore not be entirely misleading to draw a demand curve confronting the bureau, though some writers prefer to call it, more accurately, a "marginal evaluation curve";

(iv) The government or sponsoring agent is the sole buyer of the bureau's product. In conventional micro-economics terms, this appears to be a situation of bilateral monopoly. Any search for an equilibrium price and "output" may be hindered by the difficulty of modelling such factors as bargaining skill and incentive to seek agreement. Supporters of the bureaucratic paradigm have sought a way round this by claiming that the bureau benefits from the phenomenon of asymmetric information. The bureau is the sole source of information on the cost curve of its service and the cost of acquiring information on the minimum marginal and average cost curve of supplying the service is prohibitive. Apart from anything else, the bureau is in the advantageous position arising from point (ii) above that output may be very difficult to define. Some writers, following McKenzie and Tullock,[1] argue that bureaux have a better appreciation of the voters' desires for their particular service than those who represent them, simply because they are in a better position to monitor public opinion on a particular service than politicians who have to spread their interests over many different branches of government.[2]

The conventional analysis utilises these assumptions and observations in order to compare the level of output which would obtain under conditions of (i) conventional monopoly where profit maximisation is possible; (ii) the competitive solution where marginal cost = price; and (iii) the bureau optimum where maximising the size of the bureau is the sole argument in the bureaucrat's welfare function. There is clearly a strong element of artificiality in this form of comparison because the very nature of at least a fair proportion of services supplied by the public sector, namely that they are in the technical sense

1. R. B. McKENZIE and GORDON TULLOCK, *The New World of Economics*, Homewood, Ill.: Irwin, 1981.
2. See JOHN G. CULLIS and PHILIP R. JONES, 'The Economic Theory of Bureaucracy, X-Inefficiency and Wagner's Law: A Note', *Public Finance*, No. 2, 1984, pp. 191-201.

public goods, precludes their production and sale in a market.

Let us take a very simple algebraic example in which there is a downward sloping straightline marginal evaluation curve and the output of the government service is measurable and produced under conditions of long-run constant cost.

We assume that the total potential budget available to the bureau during the budget period is:

TR (total revenue) $= aQ - bQ^2$,

so that

$$MR \text{ (marginal revenue)} = \frac{dTR}{dq} = a - 2bQ.$$

The minimum total cost of producing output Q is given by

TC (total cost) $= cQ$,

so that:

CASE 1 represents the "social optimum" where marginal valuation equals marginal costs so that

$dB/dQ = dC/dQ$,
i.e. $a - 2bq = c$.

Therefore:

$$Q_o = \tfrac{1}{2}(a - c)/b. \qquad\qquad 3.1$$

CASE 2 represents the "upper bound" case for the bureau where it maximises revenue subject to movement along the minimum cost curve.

Then:

Maximise TR s.t. $TC = cQ$.
$dTR/dQ = a - 2bQ = 0$.

$$Q_u = \tfrac{1}{2}(a/b). \qquad\qquad 3.2$$

CASE 3 represents the "lower bound" case for the bureau where it is constrained by the condition that $TC = TR = B$, B being the maximum budget available.

Then: $TR = TC$.
Therefore $AQ - bQ^2 = cQ$,

$$\text{or: } Q_e = (a - c)/b. \qquad\qquad 3.3$$

The equilibrium level of Q for the bureau becomes:

$$Q \left\{ \begin{array}{l} = (a-c)/b \text{ for } a < 2c \\ = a/2b \text{ for } a > 2c \end{array} \right\}$$

$Q_u, Q_e > Q_o; \ c > 0.$

3·4

In other words, if it makes sense to identify and define the optimal solution as one where allocative efficiency is maximised, then the bureau "overproduces", but always assuming that the bureau also has an incentive to operate along its minimum cost curve.

This kind of model has been the point of departure for animated discussions on the nature of bureaucratic behaviour, and its implications for public expenditure growth, but it serves our initial purpose of taking a "Classical view" of the general approach to the economic analysis of bureaucracy. The "Classical view", as I now hope to show, anticipates much of this discussion. I return to the position of public bureaucracy in the analysis of public expenditure growth after reviewing what historical perspective can contribute to our general theme.

3. The Classical View of Bureaucracy

The most central observation to be made about the theory of bureaucracy is that bureaucrats are utility maximisers, and are thus perceived as having the same behavioural characteristics as other individual decision makers. What content should be given to the term "utility maximisation" is an important question, but at this juncture all that need be noticed is the acceptance of the view that human nature is much the same at all times and in all places.

This view is of course derived directly from the analyses of David Hume and his successor Adam Smith. Hume's famous statement that "reason is and ought only to be the slave of the passions"[1] epitomises the eighteenth century revolution in the psychological analysis of human behaviour. The word "passions" suggests dark forces at work whereas what Hume means is that our wellbeing is governed by our feelings which govern our values and our aims. The role of reason is not to determine the values of the arguments in the individual utility function and the trade-offs between them but to determine our selection of the means to maximise the function. Smith's contribution to this analysis is to demonstrate that whereas people may behave differently depending on "the situation in which they are placed",[2] they do so not because their personality changes but because the constraints under which they act to maximise their utility differ from one situation to another.

The Classical economists and their followers would therefore find themselves completely at home, and indeed could claim not merely to have anticipated but to have influenced public choice theory, though it could hardly be claimed that they were the sole root of all subsequent seminal thinking on the analysis of the motivation of public servants. Buchanan has

1. DAVID HUME, *A Treatise on Human Nature* (1739-40) in HUME, *Theory of Politics*, edited by FREDERICK WATKINS, Edinburgh: Nelson, 1951.

2. ADAM SMITH, *An Enquiry into the Nature of Causes of the Wealth of Nations* (1776). The edition quoted in the lectures is the text of the *Glasgow Edition of the Works and Correspondence of Adam Smith*, vol. 2, edited by R. H. CAMPBELL, ANDREW S. SKINNER and W. B. TODD, Oxford: Clarendon Press, 1976.

admonished Anglo-Saxon economists and political scientists by claiming that

throughout most of this century [they] continued to seem blind to what now appears so simple to us, that benevolent despots do not exist and that governmental policy emerges from a highly complex and intricate institutional structure peopled by ordinary men and women, very little different from the rest of us.[1]

It is arguable whether such sweeping condemnation is justified, but his statement, and he would surely be the first to admit it, echoes the realism of his Classical forebears.

The theory of bureaucracy also indicates that the arguments in individual utility functions may be much more extensive than simple wealth maximisation through time. Here again, Hume and Smith are quite explicit. Hume appears to take a narrower view than Smith when he states that

[nothing] is more certain than that men are, in a great measure, governed by interest, and that even when they extend their concern beyond themselves, it is not any great distance; nor is it usual for them, in common life, to look further than their nearest friends and acquaintance.[2]

In the same essay he refers to the "narrowness of soul" which makes men prefer the "present to the remote". This myopia, he argues, leads men into situations where they contradict their own interests, for what is remote is nevertheless real. The philosopher, Ernest Gellner,[3] offers a gentle parody of Hume's man with his "bundle" of feelings:

The Bundleman was a gourmet crossed with an accountant, with a touch of compassionate sensibility thrown in. He conducted his life

1. JAMES M. BUCHANAN, 'From Private Preferences to Public Philosophy: The Development of Public Choice', in *The Economics of Politics*, London: Institute of Economic Affairs, 1978, p. 4.

2. HUME, *A Treatise on Human Nature*, op. cit., III, 2. vii, 'Of the Origin of Government', p. 81. For a perceptive analysis by an Italian writer of the link between Hume's views of human nature and the origins of social institutions, see DARIO CASTIGLIONE, 'Hume's Conventionalist Analysis of Justice', *Annali della Fondazione Luigi Einaudi*, Torino, vol. XXI, 1987.

3. ERNEST GELLNER, *The Psychoanalytic Movement*, London: Paladin, 1985, p. 15.

by studying the palate and seeking to arrange for its greatest satis-faction, and his imaginative sympathy for others inclined him to favour their satisfactions, too, if to a somewhat lesser degree than his own.

In *The Theory of Moral Sentiments*,[1] Smith constructs on Hume's foundations a more articulate individual welfare function, which has attracted, interestingly enough, the attention of two con-temporary writers with a particular interest in public choice theory and bureaucracy – Musgrave[2] and Ricketts.[3] In his essay on Smith's views on distribution, Musgrave re-writes the Smithian welfare function in modern language. Let me paraphrase the arguments in such a fashion:

(i) the necessities of life (with an indication, at least, that be-yond the level of necessity the marginal utility of consumption falls);

(ii) the satisfaction gained from "beneficence", i.e. the desire to help others and to attract their approbation;

(iii) "self-esteem" in one's economic and social position; and

(iv) the satisfaction derived from being a member of an or-dered society in which "natural liberty" prevails.

Such are the many facets of Smith's position and in Mus-grave's useful disentangling job I have only one caveat to enter. Smith lays particular stress on the disutility of work and hence the importance in the individual welfare function of "ease" or "leisure".

As Ricketts sums up the position:

It is perhaps the fuller and more subtle appreciation of the nature of man as well as the more detailed attention to the institutional setting which ultimately distinguishes the study of political economy from that of economics.[4]

1. ADAM SMITH, *The Theory of Moral Sentiments*, Glasgow Edition, vol. i, edited by A. L. MACFIE and D. D. RAPHAEL, Oxford: Clarendon Press, 1976.

2. RICHARD A. MUSGRAVE, 'Adam Smith on Public Finance and Distribution', in THOMAS WILSON and ANDREW S. SKINNER, eds., *The Market and the State: Essays in Honour of Adam Smith*, Oxford: Clarendon Press, 1976, reprinted in MUSGRAVE, *Public Finance in a Democratic Society*, *op. cit.*, vol. II, pp. 260-1.

3. MARTIN RICKETTS, 'Adam Smith on Politics and Bureaucracy', in *The Economics of Politics*, *op. cit.*, pp. 171-82. My interest in this aspect of Smith's works owes much to this penetrating contribution.

4. *Ibid.*, p. 174.

That said, however, the specific contribution of the Classical economists and some of their followers to the study of bureaucracy offers a strong implicit criticism of the Niskanen/Tullock tradition. Indeed, Musgrave waves a warning finger at Libertarians who have not consulted Smith on the complexities of human nature:

Human motivation is too many sided and complex to be captured by the caricature of bureau-grabbing officials which permeates the Leviathan literature.[1]

So now we reach the point where there could be a notable divergence between the analysis of bureaucracy by Smith and others and modern public choice theorists who support the thesis of budget maximisation leading to allocative inefficiency. In a host of different places in *The Wealth of Nations*[2] and in his *Correspondence*,[3] he emphasises that if consumption is the sole end of production, then consumers will be badly serviced by those who supply goods and services under conditions where they are immune from market pressures. But he emphasises that not only will allocative efficiency be reduced, but also that it would be foolish to suppose that whatever the output it would be produced at lowest cost. His most striking examples are taken from producers in non-market situations, such as public officials, and he puzzles a great deal over the question as to how such officials, assuming that their activities cannot reasonably be privatised, are to be remunerated in a form which will promote their attention to their specified duties. More important still, given a situation where officials can ignore their duties or where these are difficult to define, an important way for increasing their welfare is through "idleness" coupled with "prodigality". Of the many examples he gives, let me refer to two typical ones.

The first makes the telling point that, as he puts it,

1. MUSGRAVE, 'Leviathan Cometh – Or Does He?, *op. cit.*, p. 209.

2. See RICKETTS, 'Adam Smith on Politics and Bureaucracy', *op. cit.*, for full documentation.

3. *The Correspondence of Adam Smith*, Glasgow Edition, vol. 6, edited by ERNEST CAMPBELL MOSSNER and IAN SIMPSON ROSS, Oxford: Clarendon Press, 1977; particularly his letter to William Cullen, pp. 173-9.

... frugality and good conduct, however, is upon most occasions, it appears from experience, sufficient to compensate, not only the private prodigality and misconduct of individuals, but the public extravagance of government. The uniform, constant and uninterrupted effort of every man to better his condition, the principle from which public and national, as well as private opulence is originally derived, is frequently powerful enough to maintain the natural progress of things toward improvement, in spite of the extravagance of government, and of the greatest errors of administration. Like the unknown principle in animal life, it frequently restores health and vigour to the constitution, in spite, not only of the disease, but of the absurd prescriptions of the doctor.[1]

The second quotation typifies a prominent concern of Smith, namely his worries concerning government attempts to engage in business. After commenting that the Post Office is the only example he can find of a mercantile pursuit which all governments can successfully manage, because, he remarks wryly, "there is no mystery in the business", he continues:

The agents of a prince regard the wealth of their master as inexhaustible; are careless at what price they buy; are careless at what price they sell; are careless at what expense they transport his goods from one place to another. Those agents frequently live with the profusion of princes, and sometimes too, in spite of that profusion, and by a proper method of making up their accounts, acquire the fortunes of princes.

Then he gives an example which should appeal to an Italian audience:

It was thus, as we are told by Machiavel, that the agents of Lorenzo of Medicis, not a prince of mean abilities, carried on his trade. The republic of Florence was several times obliged to pay the debt into which their extravagance involved him. He found it convenient, accordingly, to give up the business of merchant, the business to which his family had originally owed its fortune, and in the latter part of his life to employ both what remained of that fortune, and the revenue of the state of which he had the disposal, in projects and expenses more suitable to his station.[2]

1. ADAM SMITH, *Wealth of Nations, op. cit.*, vol. 1, Book II, iii.32, p. 343.
2. *Ibid.*, vol. 2, Book v, ii. a. 5 and 6, pp. 818-19.

You will know from Machiavelli's *History of Florence* that the wise Lorenzo shifted his investment into property!

It is very easy to dismiss the Classical analysis of human behaviour and its manifestations in non-market situations as purely descriptive and anecdotal and as conditioned by the institutional circumstances of their time. However, I hope that I have indicated how their own analysis of the evidence they produce calls in question the very restricted nature of some of the rigorous type of modelling of bureaucratic behaviour with its narrow conception of the constituents of the individual welfare function. It is also not without significance that some contemporaries of mine, such as Musgrave and Ricketts already mentioned, have seen fit to acknowledge the influence of Classical thinking. I am sure that this goes beyond a routine genuflexion to revered masters of the past coupled with a desire to offer a leaven of impressive scholarship. The Classical economists both make an offering of evidence about the actual workings of government which is interesting in its own right, if only because it suggests a search for modern parallels. They also point the way towards further developments in modelling which are worth exploring and, as I hope to show below, which shed a rather different light on the consequences of government expenditure growth than that shed by public choice analysts of today.

73

4. Bureaucracy with a Classical Utility Function

In an approach to modelling a classical utility function one is tempted to go more deeply into the question raised by Adam Smith concerning individuals and "the situation in which they are placed". Who exactly the "bureaucratic entrepreneur" is raises the same kind of questions as those encountered by micro-economists modelling the theory of the firm.[1] Just as firms may be constituted in very different ways which govern the situation in which decision makers are placed, so too will we find the same problem with governments. To try to reduce these different situations to some unique distillation of institutional assumptions and to a single behavioural model simply does not make sense.

To illustrate this problem of identifying "typical" situations, I recall my own tentative attempts in the late 1970s after a period in which I had served for three years as a senior bureaucrat in the British Government. I was asked to "model" my experiences in order for them to be compared and contrasted with US-style public choice theory and its view of bureaucracy.[2]

If only in a formal sense, the appropriate person to identify as the bureaucratic decision maker in a British context would be a Minister of the Crown in charge of a particular Department of State, who is normally a member of the Cabinet. One might encapsulate his/her welfare function in two arguments: trading off political ambition within the Government against the perceived benefits of party loyalty on which collective survival depends. This utility function would be immediately recognisable to David Hume! In maximising that function, the single-minded pursuit of budget maximisation seems inappropriate. It is true that the larger the budget, the more the individual Minister may be able to pursue policies which dramatise his actions and increase his political prestige. At the same time, the

1. For detailed consideration of this problem see MARTIN RICKETTS, *The Economics of Business Enterprise: New Approaches to the Firm*, Brighton: Wheatsheaf, 1986.
2. See my 'The Economics of Bureaucracy: An Inside View', in *The Economics of Politics, op. cit.*, pp. 117-28.

Minister will be conscious of the negative utility resulting from pushing his budget claims at the expense of other Ministers. Nor can he assume that the cross elasticity of demand for the services of his Department is low as compared to those of other Departments which may offer competing substitutes. The aim of improving public health may be attained by both better housing and better health services.

Ministers will rely on a cadre of senior public officials to prepare their budgets in accordance with government wishes. This leaves scope for considerable discretion so that decisions of such officials need not be based on the assumption of the budget constraint as a datum. The exercise of that discretion is a complex matter. A senior public official, well paid and with a secure position, seems to me to be much more concerned with maximising his reputation with his peer group, his reputation being enhanced by admiration of the clarity and persuasiveness of his drafting skill and the speed with which the machinery of government can be assembled to cope with any emergency policy matter. His "peer group", so I learnt, extended to his counterparts in major companies, often willing to "headhunt" top-rank civil servants who retire at the relatively early age nowadays of 60. There is nothing in this broad description of the utility of senior officials which points towards the single-minded pursuit of budget maximisation. This is not to say that such persons will be totally indifferent to the size and growth of their departmental budget. So far as size is concerned, some attention must be paid to preserving *una bella figura vis-à-vis* other departments and this may introduce a bias towards employment of efficient top-grade and therefore relatively well-paid staff and towards a pleasant working environment. So far as growth is concerned, the head of a major government department will resist "take-over" or absorption by another branch of government and will keep a close eye on the *relative* position in expenditure terms of his department alongside others. Both these concerns reflect the importance of maintaining reputation with one's peer group. But remembering the Classical individual welfare function, attracting the "approbation", as Adam Smith called it, of fellow members of his professional cadre, those who win in the "prestige stakes" may be able to arrange some form of compensation for the losers. In Britain this will take the form of some additional public honour or decoration.

So far I have been analysing the motivation of politicians and those who formulate their policies from which their superiors choose. The archetypal bureaucrat, at least in the popular sense, is someone whose function is to execute rather than formulate policy. Given the maxim that "many are called but few are chosen" to the higher echelons of government, those in charge of bureaux directed towards executing policies and who have to forgo the chances of promotion are subject to different constraints from their superiors. Their own level of remuneration and the pay scales of their staff are not usually under their control, which places some limit on their budgetary discretion. While they may derive positive utility from the prestige which goes with the numbers of officials under their surveillance, they can trade this off against leisure. My own contribution to the debate about the modelling of bureaucracy, for what it is worth, is the identification of bureaucratic leisure not as "off-the-job" but as "on-the-job" leisure. Bureau chiefs move down the learning curve very quickly, in my experience, leaving them the opportunity in working time to indulge in more congenial pursuits which are really leisure but can be disguised as "output". Tours to the more congenial locations of branches of government for which they are responsible, attendance at international conferences, entertainment of foreign counterparts spring readily to mind. Of course, "on-the-job leisure" normally requires complementary expenditure such as expense allowances and other perquisites of office, and the bureaucrat must have more trained staff "on line" than would otherwise be necessary to perform the tasks of his bureau, but his "satisficing" behaviour pattern limits the investment in time, energy and skill in order to maximise the size of his budget.

The essence of my contribution can be incorporated in a simple model[1] in which the first of all record the bureaucrat's utility

1. The exposition closely follows my earlier contribution: 'Public X-inefficiency: Informational and Institutional Constraints', in HORST HANUSCH, ed., *Anatomy of Government Deficiencies*, Heidelberg: Springer, 1983, pp. 125-38. See also the critique

function, remembering that he does not expect further promotion.

$$\text{Max. } U = U\ (N,L,S) \quad (U_n, U_l, U_s, > 0), \tag{3.5}$$

where

N is the number of administrative staff under his command.

L is "on-the-job" leisure measured in hours. It is easier to describe than to measure. It consists of utility-yielding activities in working hours which are rationalised as purposeful pursuits in the interests of the bureaucracy. It is clearly difficult to detect and no bureaucrat will admit that his "purposeful pursuits" fit my description.

S is the surplus or fiscal residuum over and above the wages paid to administrative staff. The higher the surplus, the easier the management of the bureau through the availability to the maximiser and his subordinates of the perquisites of office – renting better buildings, better office facilities. The argument is clearly a variant of Niskanen's "maximising the bureau budget", but it does not carry the implication that this is done by maximising the bureau's output.

There are two constraints on maximising 3.5:

$$B = wN + S. \tag{3.6}$$

B is the total budget available to the bureaucrat and is split between the wage bill and the surplus. For simplicity it is assumed that the only relevant wage bill is that of administrator grade staff and, for simplicity, they receive identical salaries. The rate w is fixed and is beyond the control of the bureaucrat.

$$L = L(N), \text{ with } L_n < 0;\ L_{nn} < 0. \tag{3.7}$$

This is the leisure constraint. The greater the size of the administrative staff, the greater the time costs of supervision and

of my own and others' attempts to elaborate the Niskanen Model by CHARLES ROWLEY and ROBERT ELGIN, 'Towards a Theory of Bureaucracy Behaviour', in DAVID GREENAWAY and G. K. SHAW, eds., *Public Choice, Public Finance and Public Policy: Essays in Honour of Alan Peacock*, Oxford: Blackwell, 1985, pp. 31-50.

control and the less the "on-the-job" leisure and the less opportunity for exploiting C^o in pursuit of leisure.
Forming the Lagrangean:

$$E = U\ (N,L,S,) + \lambda_1\ [L - L(N)] + \lambda_2\ [B - wN - S], \qquad 3.8$$

we obtain the first-order conditions for maximising 3.5 which
simplifies to:

$$U_n + U_1\ L_n = U_s w. \qquad 3.9$$

The conclusion of the model is that the bureaucrat maximises utility when the marginal utility derived from increasing N is equated
to the marginal utility derived from using the wages of marginal
increases in N for surplus (S) activities. Once N is determined,
then so is L. This represents a short-run equilibrium position.

The model obviously produces a different result from the
Niskanen model, but it is to be noted that it also differs from
other models designed to expose X-inefficiency (technical inefficiency). For example, a superficially similar preference variable in the utility function such that:

$$U = U(Q, N), \qquad 3.10$$

where Q is output and N is labour input. This is maximised
subject to $B = R(Q)$, the total budget constraint. The preference in favour of staff does mean that unit costs of bureau
production will be higher than minimum cost. However, once
the cost of labour is given, then the limitation on the demand
for labour is determined solely by the maximum size of the
budget. In the model I have presented, the increase in utility
of administration labour (N) as N increases, is offset by the
decreasing utility from the reduction in on-the-job leisure (L)
resulting from the increase in N. This places an upper limit on
the expansion of output which, given the first-order conditions,
make it possible for the output level to be below the output
produced by the profit maximising firm under conditions of pure
competition. In contrast, in both the Niskanen and Orzechowski
models, the bureaucrat "over-produces".[1]

1. WILLIAM ORZECHOWSKI, 'Economic Models of Bureaucracy: Surveys, Extensions and Evidence', in THOMAS E. BORCHERDING, ed., *Budgets and Bureaucrats: The Sources of Government Growth*, Durham, N.C.: Duke University Press, 1977, pp. 229-59.

My attempt to embody a classical utility function in a model based on my own observations in government must be treated, of course, with the reserve accorded to all such attempts. It captures only some features of the Classical view of the inefficiencies associated with discretionary behaviour within the public sector. However, like most other models of bureaucracy, it does not extend its purview to the relations between bureaucrats and those whose activities within the private sector are subject to bureaucratic regulation. In my first lecture, I made a particular point of the existence of a "policy execution" market in which it is recognised that those subject to government regulation must not be regarded as purely passive adjusters to bureaucratic action. The expansion of the public sector not only increases the opportunities for discretionary behaviour of those within government but brings with it an expansion in the points of contact with the private sector which alerts private individuals and firms to the growing influence of government on their day-to-day decisions. This is quite distinct from their concern over the goods and services provided by government which are of benefit to them and the relative efficiency in their production. Classical attention to this matter leads us to look more closely at this neglected consequence of the expanding public sector in the conclusion of this lecture.

5. *The Infection of Inefficiency*

As I have indicated, the worries expressed by public choice theorists about public sector growth are centred in the lack of control of the voting public over the discretionary activities of politicians and public officials which results in both growing allocative inefficiency (voters' choices are not reflected in the composition of public expenditure) and in growing X-inefficiency (services are provided at above minimum cost), both of which exacerbate the distributional struggle. In addition, a growing proportion of voters become public employees which suggests a concomitant change in voters' preferences in favour of publicly provided goods. The confrontation of citizens and government is confined to one instrument of political participation – control (or lack of it) of the legislature.

The trouble with this approach is that it assumes a dichotomy between the public and private sector with the main link between the two being the political system as conventionally defined. Politicians are "go-betweens" between voters and bureaucrats. This displays the vestigial influence of the conventional welfare economics paradigm in which the individual producer or consumer takes the market situation with which he is confronted more or less as given, and government actions are autonomous.

I realised at the time that I made this criticism that there was a marked contrast between this approach and that of the Classical economists and, on re-reading what they had to say, I am more than ever struck by their perspicacity. Their concern, so far as the behaviour of public servants was concerned, was not simply that it was discretionary and resulted in inefficient service but was directed towards the study of the relations not between bureaucrats and the legislature but between bureaucrats and the public. As already indicated, Smith's work is riddled with references to the "want of parsimony" in public spending leading to loose contracting arrangements with private suppliers.[1] In his theory of taxation, he does not assume that tax-

---

1. ADAM SMITH, *Wealth of Nations, op. cit.*, vol. 2, Book v, iii, p. 909.

payers are merely Pavlovian dogs. If taxes become oppressive, as they will be perceived if they increase *pari passu* with expenditure, the taxpayer has to consider how far his interests entail compliance:

The law, contrary to all the ordinary principles of justice, first creates the temptation, and then punishes those who yield to it; and it commonly enhances the punishment too in proportion to the very circumstance which ought certainly to alleviate it, the temptation to commit the crime.[1]

We find an echo of the confrontation between citizens and government in Bentham:

... attend an agent for government and think whether anything in private life can equal the indifference with which he treats your business, although, or rather because it is public business, even when he is best disposed towards it.[2]

Of course, these isolated quotations do not add up to a coherent analysis of the economic relationships between the bureaucracy and the public. They are nevertheless consistent with the thesis that an interpretation of the growth of the public sector as an indication of the reduction in "market failure" by the provision of public goods and public regulations (e.g. pollution measures) to reduce negative externalities is incomplete. No account is taken, not only of the neglect of the opportunities for discretionary action by public officials, but also of the private sector's opportunities for discretionary action in their transactions with government.

I have dealt with this subject *in extenso* elsewhere[3] but a few words are perhaps in order as a link with my final lecture. The growing dominance of the government as a buyer in certain markets as it grows in size must encourage the growth in counter-

---

1. *Ibid.*, vol. 2, Book v, ii.b, pp. 826-7.
2. JEREMY BENTHAM, 'A Plan for Augmentation of the Revenue', in *Jeremy Bentham's Economic Writings, op. cit.*, vol. II, pp. 115-49.
3. ALAN T. PEACOCK, 'On the Anatomy of Government Failure', *Public Finance*, vol. 32, No. 1, 1980, pp. 33-4.

vailing power through merger of suppliers or through the extension of unionisation amongst government employees. It may be in the interests of bureaucrats to encourage this growth in market imperfection, for it may become simpler and more convenient to negotiate with a few dominant suppliers. In addition, as private enterprises and, indeed, private individuals become more dependent on government, they will have a strong incentive to invest in activities which improve their bargaining skills in government. In Britain, a common form of such investment is to attract experienced, not necessarily retired, public officials who both know how the government machine works and how to direct its operation towards favouring particular enterprises. Compliance costs with legislation may be reduced by negotiation over the application of such legislation which may give officials considerable discretion. Government departments frequently face the "adverse selection" problem in cases where they offer subsidies to firms in the name of positive externalities because the sole effective source of information on the potential performance of the enterprise will be the enterprise itself. In short, the asymmetric information difficulty encountered in checking whether or not the bureaucrat is fooling his masters is paralleled in the relation between the bureaucrat and his suppliers.

In the next lecture I shall consider how public choice theorists have applied their analysis to the problems encountered in trying to reduce or at least contain the size of the public sector. Their approach is primarily normative. Welfare criteria are defined and the appropriate fulfilment of these criteria is reflected in proposals for constitutional and administrative reform. In this respect, the contributions of the Swedish economists, Wicksell and Lindahl, and of several of their Italian contemporaries are particularly important. However, I think it would be an abrogation of responsibility to devise reforms the implementation of which appears to depend on the waving of a magic wand. A more difficult, daunting but absorbing task is trying to devise recommendations for reduction or containment of the public sector which have some chance of being accepted in an economic system in which the interests of the various bargaining groups are diverse and frequently opposed to one another. To come anywhere near a solution to this problem requires us to recognise the forces at play which the Classical economists so vividly described and analysed.

FOURTH LECTURE

The Calculus of Consent and Limits on Government Expenditure Growth

1. Introduction. – 2. The Justification for Constitutional Change. – 3. The Case for a Balanced Budget Constraint. – 4. Tax Limitation and the Wicksellian Tradition. – 5. Epilogue.

1. Introduction

In this lecture I propose to illustrate my thesis with reference to the perennial question of how to place limits on the growth of the public sector. In contemporary language employed by public choice theorists we are concerned with the problem of "the taming of Leviathan".[1]

I shall avoid evaluating normative systems which are commonly used to confer a badge of legitimacy on particular kinds of policy measures or constitutional arrangements employed by Leviathan tamers. I shall however consider the normative origins of such measures or arrangements, if only because these are of particular significance to those public choice theorists concerned about the Leviathan problem. To be more specific, public choice theorists who have placed particular emphasis on allying their normative prescriptions with Paretian type welfare economics derive their policy recommendations from the fulfilment of voters' choices in which voters have as complete information as possible about the consequences of their decisions. Two major lines of constitutional change are recommended by them. The first is to rid the political system of what may be termed "the tyranny of the median voter" and to maximise the degree of consent to budgetary changes, subject to the constraints imposed by transaction costs.[2] The second is to reduce

---

1. As Musgrave points out, the term is associated with the predispositions of "minimum-state" liberals. See MUSGRAVE, 'Leviathan Cometh – Or Does He?', *op. cit.*

2. In terms of our historical perspective thesis, this explains the choice of KNUT WICKSELL's work. See, particularly, his *Finanztheoretische Untersuchungen, op. cit.*

the prevalence of "fiscal illusion" which enables governments to distort the information available to taxpayers/voters about the consequences of their decisions.[1]

1. The first fullest expression of this view is attributed to AMILCARE PUVIANI. See his *Teoria della illusione finanziaria* (1903), edited by FRANCO VOLPI, Milano: ISEDI, 1973. I have benefited considerably from Professor Volpi's scholarly introduction to Puviani's work.

2. The Justification for Constitutional Change

The contemporary justification for emphasising constitutional change as a method for limiting government expenditure growth can be explained as follows:

(i) As already pointed out in Lecture 2, there appear to be no effective built-in incentives to curb expenditure growth of the kind which could operate in private markets. Even if a majority of taxpayers/voters preferred to see a reduction in the G/GDP ratio, they are beset by the isolation paradox. They may be uncertain whether, if they so vote, that the outcome of the political decision-making process would produce a quid pro quo in the form of a reduction in their tax burdens. As voters do not pay directly for government services and their contributions in the form of tax payments need bear little relationship to the benefits that they hope to derive from such services, they have a strong incentive to vote for politicians who will maximise their gains from government and minimise their tax burdens;

(ii) It follows from (i) that there will be strong pressures on vote maximising politicians to resolve the dilemma created by utility maximising voters by support for debt-financed public expenditure. The disputed question as to whether there is an equivalence between debt and tax financing must be addressed before one can judge the rationality of this form of political action. It forms an important element in my later commentary on the role of historical perspective in appraising methods of controlling public expenditure growth. For the moment, I simply accept the assertion that debt financing lowers taxpayers' resistance to cuts in public spending. Then the concern of those who argue for constitutional change as a necessary condition for preventing Leviathan going on the rampage is more readily understood;

(iii) Although commanding widespread political support, schemes to cut the growth in public spending by eliminating X-inefficiency have built-in resistances to their promotion and execution. I have supported this position elsewhere by exploring the analogy with attempts to eliminate X-inefficiency in the private sector by anti-monopoly action.[1] In the first place, anti-monopoly action by government will only be given "teeth" to the extent that there is a strong consumer interest in eliminating monopolistic practices. The arguments in (i) and (ii) above hardly suggest that "consumers" of government services have both a common and effective as well as a sustained interest in combating such practice in government services, be they politicians or taxpayers. Apart from the isolation paradox problem, there is the additional barrier of the interests of government employees themselves, mindful both of the effects of eliminating X-inefficiency on their employment prospects and of their position as voters. In the second place, any government body landed with the task of detecting and eliminating X-inefficiency is in a much more difficult and sensitive position *vis-à-vis* those government departments under investigation. In the private sector, there is a presumption that once some restrictive practices have been declared illegal, the problem is to establish their existence. Once a particular case of such practices is detected, a precedent may be set which forces companies adopting similar practices to abandon them or at least to consider very carefully whether they wish to incur the costs of a legal battle. In the public sector, however, it is inconceivable that any branch of government will not have obtained legal sanction for its activities through legislative approval of its budget and compliance with accounting and audit rules. Eliminating X-inefficiency will depend on what are likely to be fundamental political changes requiring the "death" of the bureau or its take-over by another branch of government or by putting out a major part of its services to private tender. The inevitably high political profile of change will alert the many interest groups to the consequences of measures designed to eliminate X-inefficiency for their members. Even if there is general agreement that investigation of restrictive practices in government departments is desirable, the strong likelihood that limited resources will be made available to conduct

1. See PEACOCK, 'Public X-Inefficiency', *op. cit.*

such investigation will make the setting of orders or priority for investigation a "hot" political issue. The final order of priority may not be closely correlated with the expected prevalence of X-inefficiency in different departments. That will depend on which other policy matters are being traded at Cabinet level, on the bargaining skill of the Ministers in charge of departments, and on the position of individual Ministers in the Cabinet hierarchy;

(iv) It must be taken as axiomatic by public choice theorists that each adult member of the community has equal voting rights, whatever the decision rule which is chosen to give effect to those rights. This precludes any recommendations which would narrow the exercise of the franchise as a way of reversing the "de Tocqueville effect" – certainly not a recommendation one could derive from de Tocqueville himself! (Hugh Dalton, one of the few British public finance specialists with a knowledge of Italian writing in his subject and, of course, a famous British Chancellor of the Exchequer, once told my seminar at the London School of Economics that the only solution to the reduction of public social services expenditure in the United Kingdom was to disenfranchise those who had reached pensionable age – like himself!). A related question of parenthetic interest is the exercise of voting rights by public employees and, by extension, their right to be members of the legislature. Certainly, some public choice theorists[1] have been concerned about these questions and have suggested that public employees should vote in separate constituencies and should not be able to be members of legislative bodies which also employ them. I take it as read that such suggestions are subsidiary to those which rely on major constitutional provisions.

This prelude to the consideration of methods of curbing the strength of Leviathan which are of particular concern to "constitutionalists" is designed more to explain rather than to justify their emphasis on constitutional reform. While a good case could be made for the claim that such reforms are a precondition for the

---

1. See, for example, GORDON TULLOCK, *The Vote Motive*, London: Institute of Economic Affairs, 1976.

successful pursuit of the alternative recommendations considered in (iii) and (iv) above, it remains to be argued whether constitutional reforms have a better chance of being implemented. However, this issue, while an important one, is not germane to our main theme. The demand for historical perspective as a factor in influencing ideas about the control of Leviathan happens to be much more clearly discerned in the area of constitutional reform than in other areas.

3. The Case for a Balanced Budget Constraint

The case for a balanced budget constraint as a method for controlling the growth of public spending emanates from the proposition of Buchanan and Wagner[1] that the replacement of current tax financing by government borrowing has the effect of reducing the perceived price of goods supplied by the government. This implies that taxpayers do not anticipate the future tax liability which current borrowing entails. Taxpayers therefore underestimate the "price" of government-supplied goods and the demand for them is accordingly increased. The policy implication must be that constitutional limits have to be placed on government borrowing for all layers of government if the "true" price of government expenditure is to be registered with voters/taxpayers.

The first striking thing about this proposition is that it is clearly at variance with the "debt-neutrality hypothesis" which has restored Ricardo to his rightful place as the inspirer of the revival of interest in Neo-Classical debt theory.[2] The essential elements of this hypothesis are well known. When a government issues debt finance instead of levying taxes of the same amount, individuals presumably perceive that additional future taxes will have to be raised in order for the debt interest to be paid. The future taxes discounted at the debt interest rate will have an equal present value with the taxes which could have been levied to finance current expenditure so that the timing of tax liabilities will have a neutral effect on the wealth of the taxpayer. It seems reasonable to conclude, therefore, that the method of finance of government expenditure will have no effect *per se* on the demand

---

1. BUCHANAN and WAGNER, *Democracy in Deficit, op. cit.*; see also BUCHANAN, ROWLEY and TOLLISON, eds., *Deficits, op. cit.*, particularly Chapters 1, 11, and 12.
2. DAVID RICARDO, *Works and Correspondence, op. cit.*, vol. IV, *Pamphlets and Papers, 1815-1823*, Cambridge: Cambridge University Press, 1951, pp. 186-87. See also, GEOFFREY H. BRENNAN and JAMES M. BUCHANAN, 'The Logic of the Ricardian Equivalence Theorem', in BUCHANAN, ROWLEY and TOLLISON, eds., *Deficits, op. cit.*, pp. 79-92. For discussion of the Italian debate on the Ricardian position, see GIUSEPPE EUSEPI, 'A Contribution to the Theory of Public Debt', Paper presented to the European Public Choice Society, Reggio Calabria, April 1987 (mimeo).

for government-supplied goods. It is not necessary to enter the interesting debate which has emanated from the discussion of the precise conditions which must be fulfilled if the Ricardian equivalence hypothesis is to hold. Two caveats are germane to our argument and make a useful prelude to further evidence of the importance of historical perspective in the balanced budget debate. The most obvious concerns individuals' expectations as to when the debt will be paid. Clearly, individuals will have a distinct preference for debt issue over tax payments if future obligations to pay debt extend beyond their lifetime, though this caveat, too, raises the further question of the extent to which welfare of future generations enters into the utility functions of current voters/taxpayers who have to choose or approve the tax/debt mix. The second caveat concerns the implicit assumption that the taxpayer has perfect foresight and complete information which enables him to forecast accurately the timing and amount of repayment which he shall bear. A related point is that the taxpayer may be able to exercise some influence on the distribution of the future tax burden, if not on the total amount, by avoidance devices which affect the distribution of his taxable income through time and by more positive influences on the choice of the type and distribution of taxes which are within the play of fiscal politics. Opportunistic behaviour by some individuals means, in Buchanan's terminology, that an individual's liability is contingent on the behaviour of others. The only protection against "irresponsible" behaviour is to favour the use of tax finance over deficit finance.

It will come as no surprise to hear that the debate about debt neutrality remains unresolved, even when empirical testing is attempted.[1] What is noticeable, as soon as one attempts to bring it within a public choice framework, is that the contingency liability argument assumes that the tax/debt mix will depend solely on voter behaviour, with politicians and governments as

1. For a discussion of the problems of empirical investigations of debt illusion, see ILDE RIZZO and ALAN T. PEACOCK, 'Government Debt and Growth in Public Spending', *Public Finance*, No. 2, 1987, pp. 285-91. But see also the reply to this article by HIROFUMI SHIBATA and YOKO KIMURA in the same issue of that journal, pp. 292-6.

passive adjusters to their wishes. The active involvement of governments in pursuing their interests adds a new dimension as they are the initiators of the tax/debt "agenda". Following Buchanan's most recent formulation of the Buchanan/Wagner hypothesis, one begins with a situation where there is budgetary equilibrium under a balanced budget,[1] that is to say constituency pressures for an increase in public expenditure are exactly balanced by pressures for reduced rates of taxation such that there is a political equilibrium:[2]

Let us now impose on this equilibrium a "new technology" of government borrowing. Political agents will treat this new technology as a shift outward in their feasibility space, since they can now respond favourably to constituency pressures for more outlays without offsetting pressures against tax increases. So long as constituencies respond less negatively to debt issue than to taxation over some range, the result must hold.[3]

A new political equilibrium must be established where constituency pressures produce a balance between expanded outlays and the combined levy of taxes and the issue of new debt.

It will be noted that there are two important ideas about the characteristics of government colouring Buchanan's proposition – the "countervailing power" which government can use in determining the revenue "mix" and the form in which that power will be exercised. Both these ideas illustrate my main thesis – the permeation of public choice theory not only with echoes from past generations of thinkers but with ideas of such thinkers which have maintained their potency. Both these ideas are derived from Italian writing and, while this will be clear to this audience nurtured on such writing, they bear some repetition and acknowledgment on the part of a *straniero*. Moreover, it

---

1. JAMES M. BUCHANAN, 'Budgetary Bias in Post-Keynesian Politics: The Erosion and Potential Replacement of Fiscal Norms', in BUCHANAN, ROWLEY and TOLLISON, eds., *Deficits, op. cit.,* pp. 180-95.

2. In the sense described by GARY BECKER in his seminal article 'A Theory of Competition among Pressure Groups for Political Influence', *Quarterly Journal of Economics,* August 1983, pp. 371-400.

3. BUCHANAN, 'Budgetary Bias in Post-Keynesian Politics', *op. cit.,* p. 182.

should be of interest to Italians to observe which of the many fruitful ideas on questions of public finance theory have taken root elsewhere and what comments and criticisms have accompanied their development.

The first idea is derived from the long and intensive discussion of Italian writers concerning the nature of the fiscal decision-making process. In its modern form it began with the examination of Austrian marginalist ideas concerning the satisfaction of collective needs, and of analogical methods of reasoning which tried to draw a parallel between individual and collective decision making. The former idea was an attack on the one-sidedness of the Austrian theory which, in Montemartini's words, "relates only to the conditions of demand for public services and not to the conditions of supply".[1] Whatever the normative underpinnings of marginalism with its emphasis on individual satisfaction, the need for coercion as the inevitable accompaniment of collective decision making, presupposes knowledge of how coercion is used and the consequences of that use. The latter idea as a guide to how governments are constructed and how they actually behave was soon dispensed with once one examined the various forms which government could take, for implicitly, an analogy between individual and government "housekeeping" confined attention to government as a single decision maker – a dictator. As Buchanan himself acknowledged at an early stage in the development of his own ideas on public choice,[2] a whole succession of writers including Pantaleoni, Mazzola, De Viti de Marco, Puviani and Fasiani – to name only the more prominent – emphasised that the state was not some organic whole independent of the individuals who composed it. Its composition and powers would vary in time and place depending on which economic group formed the "political enter-

1. GIOVANNI MONTEMARTINI, 'Le basi fondamentali di una scienza finanziaria pura', *Giornale degli Economisti*, 1900, II, pp. 555-76. Translated as 'The Fundamental Principles of a Pure Theory of Public Finance', in MUSGRAVE and PEACOCK, eds., *Classics in the Theory of Public Finance, op. cit.*, pp. 137-51.

2. See his 'La Scienza delle finanze: The Italian Tradition in Fiscal Theory', in JAMES M. BUCHANAN, *Fiscal Theory and Political Economy: Selected Essays*, Chapel Hill, N.C.: University of North Carolina Press, 1960, pp. 24-74.

prise", as Montemartini termed it, offering public services. A kind of typology of political enterprises was called for, ranging from an individual sovereign or autocracy with extensive powers over those who supplied resources for collective use to the case where the entire community constituted the enterprise.

Compared with their Scandinavian counterparts, the influence of this approach to the study of public choice problems is relatively late in the day though the work of Pantaleoni and De Viti de Marco has been available in translation for many years. One explanation offered is the emotional resistance of English-language scholars to a fiscal theory which was based on the fiscal behaviour of a "ruling class".[1] If Kayaalp's explanation is valid then it would be paradoxical if it implied some kind of condonation of the forms of government which the Italian writers put under their microscopes. So far as positive theory is concerned, the "unpalatable" nature of the Italian approach may originate in scepticism at the difficulties encountered in applying economic analysis to group behaviour, as the typology of "political enterprises" required. So far as normative theory is concerned, it would be a travesty of the position of writers such as De Viti and Pantaleoni that, because they showed that coercion was a necessary condition for decision making in government, they were not concerned as to how coercion would be used. But this is a side-issue. The important thing is that we have come to learn through the Italian *Scienza delle Finanze*, in its various manifestations, that the study of the supply side of political decision making is essential if we are to understand why government has grown and, possibly, how such growth might be halted.

The importance of recognising the supply side influences on government growth is a kind of missing element in the debate about whether taxpayers make rational decisions in the light of uncertainty about their future tax burdens resulting from debt issue. The debate, as usually conducted, does not assume that any information, such as can be provided by government,

---

1. As made by ORHAN KAYAALP, 'Public Choice Elements of the Italian Theory of Public Goods', *Public Finance*, No. 3, 1985, pp. 395-410.

is denied to the taxpayer or that there is any incentive for government to present it in a misleading form. A taxpayer/voter may correctly perceive that an increase in current expenditure financed by debt issue does not bring with it an inevitable fiscal equivalent in tax burdens. However, a government anxious to remain in power, and perceiving growth in public spending as a means for doing so, has a strong incentive to create and to foster the illusion that methods of revenue raising are less onerous to taxpayers than they are really likely to be. It will also have the power to control both the amount of information and the form in which it is presented, such that the individual taxpayer would incur relatively high costs in being able to assess its accuracy. The development and illustration of this thesis is, of course, the unique contribution of Amilcare Puviani.[1] It may seem paradoxical to Italian economists that of all the great figures in Italian public finance, he is the one whose work most often offers the point of departure of a major item in contemporary fiscal debate in the English language, all the more paradoxical because an English translation has so far not appeared in print.

Puviani's analysis of government behaviour consonant with these last observations covers a wide range of techniques of which "debt illusion" is only a part, and not necessarily the most cogently argued part of his analysis. If I am critical of this analysis and its use by those who have derived inspiration from it, one must bear in mind that one is only concerned with a small piece of his general thesis. There are two parts to his analysis. The first concerns the taxpayer's perception of the debt/tax alternative in which he accepts the Ricardian equivalence thesis. However, there is another element in the taxpayer's utility function which, at the margin, will make him favour debt issue as a method of finance. This is that the individual feels himself more in control over his portfolio of assets and their capital value if he does not have to pay taxes presently, even though the liability incurred by public debt is fully offset by the capitalised value of future taxes. Here the illusion is of the taxpayer's own

---

1. PUVIANI, *Teoria della illusione finanziaria, op. cit.*, Chapter 3, Section 16.

making, and the government can take advantage of this. The second concerns the ways in which the government itself can induce the taxpayer to believe that the debt obligations are less onerous than they are. These obligations may be disguised by reliance on the complexity that the government can introduce into the structure of the debt by issues of debt of different maturities, different types of securities and different yields. If we extend the definition of public debt to cover currency creation, then it becomes very difficult for the individual taxpayer to identify his share of the "costs" of being subjected to inflationary finance.

A very interesting example of the use of Puviani's speculations in order to clarify the issue of how taxpayers perceive future debt service taxes is provided by Cavaco-Silva.[1] Consider the following definition of "debt illusion":

$$k_t = 1 - \frac{A'_t}{A_t} \qquad (A_t > 0), \qquad\qquad 4.1$$

where k_t is the degree of debt illusion of an individual at the beginning of time t;

A_t = present value of total future taxes required to service the debt;

A'_t = present value of total taxes as perceived by the individual.

(Both A_t and A'_t are discounted at the same rate of interest.)

Clearly if $A'_t = A_t$, there is no debt illusion, for $k_t = 0$. If $A'_t > A_t$ there is positive illusion. As $A'_t \longrightarrow 0$, then $k_t \longrightarrow 1$, i.e. we approach a situation of total debt illusion.

To say that the individual suffers from debt illusion does not preclude him taking some view of what his share of future debt service taxes will be, though he may be uncertain of the amount.

1. ANIBAL A. CAVACO-SILVA, *Economic Effects of Public Debt*, London: Martin Robertson, 1977, pp. 37-40.

In other words, any error in estimating his share of future debt service taxes is not solely dependent on debt illusion. The estimate made by the individual may be calculated as follows:

$$a'_t = h'_t \, A'_t \qquad (A'_t > 0), \qquad\qquad 4.2$$

where A'_t is defined as before, and h'_t is the individual's perception of his share in the debt service tax liability. By substitution in (4.1) we get

$$a'_t = h'_t \, (1 - k_t) \, A_t, \qquad\qquad 4.3$$

which indicates how the individual's estimated tax share depends on the degree of tax illusion.

Cavaco-Silva performs a useful service in making a firm distinction between the individual's degree of illusion about the discounted value of future debt service taxes and how the individual makes any consequential calculations about his personal liability which involves decision making under conditions of uncertainty. He is concerned with making sense of the logic of the debt illusion hypothesis, but his formulation may be used to cast doubt on the Puviani supposition that debt illusion is positive, i.e. $k_t > 0$. The individual may delude himself by believing that he is in more control of his assets if he pays debt service taxes in the future as an alternative to paying taxes to finance current expenditures. However, why should the second arm of Puviani's argument, namely the government's control over the complexity of the debt structure and maturity, require that the individual is deluded into believing that debt issue is less rather than more onerous than the equivalent payment in taxes? Of course, I suppose that Puviani's whole battery of methods by which government can delude taxpayers may lessen general resistance to any method by which revenue is raised.

The other worry I have is that the taxpayer seems to be in a state of permanent "fiscal anaesthesia", to use Cavaco-Silva's preferred alternative description of the condition of illusion. It may be supposed that k_t is not independent of A_t in equation (4.3), such that k_t diminishes as A_t increases. A rise in the total tax burden may induce the taxpayer to incur the costs of acquiring more information about the effect of the fiscal system on his economic position. Gandenberger[1] has extended this argument in a rather different way. Voters need not only form expectations about present deficits and borrowing but also about future deficits and borrowing and may take the former expectation as an indication of the latter. Both the relative size of the deficit and its growth are conventionally regarded as portents of economic instability, particularly in recent years in Western countries, thus engendering growing concern at the growth in public expenditure as the primary source of that instability. Gandenberger identifies public debt illusion with the inability of taxpayers to distinguish between endogenous (cyclical) and exogenous (structural) components of the growth in borrowing. The "marginal tax-price of government services" may be misperceived when taxpayers mistake a fall in the deficit produced by an upturn in the cycle and its effects on tax revenues as a permanent fall in the deficit. Taking advantage of this misperception may be very tempting to politicians who see it as an opportunity for increasing public expenditures which move their popularity function in the right direction. Gandenberger does not mention Puviani in the course of his exposition, but his alternative version of debt illusion is fully consistent with Puviani's line of reasoning. Like the illusionist on the stage, governments can substitute new techniques of fiscal illusion as old ones are "seen through" by the audience.

We may be left in some doubt, therefore, about the generality of the Buchanan/ Wagner hypothesis. Nor are we likely to find much to help us make up our minds by a review of the empirical testing of the hypothesis.[2] However, if we assume that reducing deficits could at least be a contributory factor in attempts to control government expenditure growth, then the end implies the means – some form of budget rule which constrains governments by determining borrowing limits. There is an enormous literature on this subject, much of it recently generated by the worries surrounding the federal deficit in the United States, and

1. OTTO GANDENBERGER, 'On Government Borrowing and False Political Feedback', in HERBER, ed., *Public Finance and Public Debt, op. cit.*, pp. 205-16.
2. See Footnote 1, p. 92.

which I do not propose to review.[1] There are two general points to be made in this context. The first is that the desirability of a constitutional requirement which insists on a balanced budget presupposes that there are no circumstances in which policy aims would require the incurring of deficits, although some element of flexibility would be necessary if only because of forecasting uncertainties. Anyone who contends that fiscal policy has a role to play in economic stabilisation is not going to accept that proposition, or at least will insist that budget balance must be over the period of the business cycle, if this cycle can be identified. The second is more germane to the general Puviani position, and concerns the feasibility of defining budget balance so that any infringement of both the spirit and the letter of the law can be prevented.

The application of the Puviani thesis suggests that governments faced with demand for constitutional amendment to tie their hands by budget balance provisions will have ample opportunities to practise the art of fiscal illusion:

(i) Disagreements about the definition of the scope of budget balance can be exploited. The definition could be narrow, only applying to government consumption and transfer expenditure to be financed by taxes, or wide, including not only capital expenditure but all manner of off-budget expenditure (public enterprises' capital expenditure) and state social security funds. The search costs incurred in finding out precisely what every government agency does and the legal sanction which governs its operations may be prohibitive for the constitutional reformer. Reliance has to be placed on the information supplied by an interested party – a bureaucracy not likely to want its hands tied by a balanced budget condition;

(ii) Once it is decided which institutions are within the scope of a balanced budget condition, it may still be possible for the letter of budget balance rule to be adhered to and its spirit violated. This may be done by reclassifying budget items. There will be ample scope for this if the rule only applies to current

1. See BUCHANAN, ROWLEY and TOLLISON, eds., *Deficits*, *op. cit.*, Part II.

expenditure but not to capital expenditure or if there are escape clauses covering exceptions to the rule, such as some national emergency provision. Given also the normal delay in the presentation of full government accounts, the detection of various forms of statistical legerdemain may be both difficult and dilatory, with the fiscal authorities in a position to argue about the details from a position of strength;

(iii) Budget balance can be achieved by adjusting taxes as well as expenditure. The Puviani thesis suggests that a shift from debt to tax financing does not necessarily mean that the fiscal authorities are powerless to prevent the revelation of a rise in the perceived price of government services. This is to underestimate their ingenuity in disguising the impact of an increase in taxation, for example by relying on taxes whose increase in yield does not necessarily require an adjustment in tax rates.

Nothing in what I have said is designed to do anything more than to indicate the deep permeation of the public choice analysis of fiscal politics by a series of important insights and suggestions offered by Puviani. So far as the budget rule is concerned, these insights and suggestions make it clear that countering the existence of debt illusion by removing its *modus vivendi*, the issue of debt itself, still leaves open the possibility that the fiscal authorities, *if instructed to do so*, can employ other methods for trying to keep taxpayers in a state of more or less permanent "fiscal anaesthesia". I make no prediction as to whether such methods will work and clearly whether governments will find it expedient to employ them.

Senator Muskie once stated that

we don't need fiscal handcuffs to wipe the deficit out. We need fiscal discipline. If we have that will, no formula is necessary. If we don't, no formula will work.[1]

I am sure that those who support a balanced budget provision would admit that creating the climate in which such a provision is acceptable is an important prerequisite for its success.

---

1. Quoted in *Proposal for a Constitutional Convention to Require a Balanced Budget*, Washington, D.C.: American Enterprise Institute, 1979, p. 26.

Furthermore, they would argue that such a provision does not preclude the institution of other constitutional reforms which promote the same end of keeping public expenditure and Leviathan under control. One of such reforms I now consider in some detail.

4. *Tax Limitation and the Wicksellian Tradition*[1]

The importance of the concept of budget balance to "contractarian" public choice analysts is that it is an important contributory factor for aiding rational choice by taxpayers. This is because, as we have shown at some length, recourse to borrowing by government places a veil over the tax-price structure such that taxpayers are not fully aware of the consequences of their actions as they affect themselves and as they may affect future taxpayers, including their heirs, whose welfare may be an argument in their own welfare functions. However, whether or not the balanced budget condition would produce a closer awareness of the consequences of their actions, there is no guarantee, even if it did, that voters/taxpayers would be constrained by the process of fiscal exchange to equate the marginal cost of what they are willing to pay for government services with the marginal benefit. How close will be the correspondence between marginal cost and benefit for all voters will depend on the decision rule governing the size and composition of the government budget.

Although this conclusion must be obvious to this audience, it seems to me worthwhile to spend a little time in elaborating the way in which this problem is usually presented to us. In the pure public goods case where goods are "non-rival in consumption", the same amount is consumed by all. However, with differences in income and in tastes and preferences, the marginal rates of substitution are no longer the same, that is to say that if individuals by some method had to reveal their preferences, they would offer a different tax-price for the same amount of the good. Were it possible to identify a demand schedule we would

1. The following section was written before the appearance of Professor Wagner's perceptive essay on Wicksell which clearly demonstrates Wicksell's continuing influence on the discussion of present-day issues of public choice analysis. It is particularly valuable for its study of the links between Swedish fiscal history and Wicksell's proposal for constitutional reform. His essay illustrates very clearly my thesis concerning the shift of emphasis over the last thirty years in what I have called the "inspirational content" of Wicksell's work. See RICHARD E. WAGNER, 'The Calculus of Consent: A Wicksellian Retrospective', *Public Choice*, February 1988, pp. 153-66.

have to sum the marginal rates of substitution vertically, and, to obtain a solution, those wishing to consume the social good would have to be prepared to pay different prices, for the requirement for an "efficient solution" would be that the marginal rates of substitution in consuming the good must equal the marginal rate of transformation in its production. This conclusion is the modern translation of the famous partial equilibrium analysis of Lindahl,[1] into a general equilibrium setting. However, in the words of Samuelson, while a "solution 'exists'; the problem is how to 'find' it".[2] Finding a solution, of course, runs up against the difficulty of how to deal with the problem of non-revelation of preferences. Ignoring the small numbers case, the pressure on individuals to reveal their preferences must be progressively lowered as the numbers rise, leaving each individual speculating on the possibility of the social good being supplied at little or no cost to himself. I am still surprised, though it is still common practice, at the enormous investment undertaken by economists in devising solutions to the preference revelation problem which presupposes that dictated solutions are both desirable and feasible. It is amazing to me how often it is taken for granted that if by some miraculous device, all preferences for social goods could be known, including registered changes in individuals' preferences systems, an imposed solution is then considered justified. Any argument in favour of the individual's property rights in political participation must then be ignored or its consequences too horrible to contemplate, given the (arguable) possibility that majority vote decision rules may violate the Arrow conditions for a rational voting constitution.[3]

From the very beginning of "contractarian" public choice theory, the influence of Wicksell has been a dominant one, as instanced in the statement by James Buchanan, incidentally

1. LINDAHL, *Die Gerechtigkeit der Besteuerung, op. cit.* The relevant analysis is translated as 'Just Taxation – A Positive Solution', in MUSGRAVE and PEACOCK, eds., *Classics in the Theory of Public Finance, op. cit.,* pp. 168-76.

2. PAUL A. SAMUELSON, 'Diagrammatic Exposition of a Theory of Public Expenditure', *Review of Economics and Statistics*, November 1955, pp. 350-6.

3. For a critical review of the Arrow approach, see ROWLEY and PEACOCK, *Welfare Economics*, Chapter 2.

Wicksell's translator,[1] that "my own emphasis was on modelling politics-as-exchange, under the acknowledged major influence of Knut Wicksell's great work in Public Finance".[2] Wicksell took it as self-evident that the moral imperative of choice was provided in "voluntary consent", with consent implying universal suffrage and representative government. One is inclined to forget that this imperative and its implications were radical views in his day. Not only did he believe in this version of democracy, but he criticised contemporary writers who took it as axiomatic that a "just" tax system postulated some form of benevolent despotism.[3] At least such writers could offer the excuse that such a form of government was a positive fact, whatever position might be taken by them on questions of political philosophy, whereas their modern counterparts seeking an "ethical observer" to solve the problem of free riding, simply conjure up this artefact from their imaginations. Wicksell therefore saw his task as follows:

[instead] of expecting guidance from a doctrine of taxation that is based on the political philosophy of by-gone ages, it should endeavour to unlock the mysteries of the spirit of progress and development. The movement that is afoot cannot be stopped, but it might be guided in a direction such that the desired goal is fully attained to the satisfaction of all.[4]

We all know what a formidable task Wicksell set himself. Maximising consent meant seeking a budget decision which in its size and composition of expenditure and taxes reflected unanimity as near as possible. This required first of all a distinct rule of budgetary procedure – the simultaneous determination of both expenditure and the means for covering its cost. What is interesting is that Wicksell had independently seen the importance of tax illusion, for he observed that in Sweden the buoyancy of the yield of indirect taxes gave governments the opportunity to claim that the necessary means for financing

1. See WICKSELL, 'A New Principle of Just Taxation', *op. cit.*
2. BUCHANAN, 'Budgetary Bias in Post-Keynesian Politics', *op. cit.*
3. WICKSELL, 'A New Principle of Just Taxation', *op. cit.*, pp. 82-3.
4. *Ibid.*, p. 87.

increased expenditure did not require invoking the simultaneity rule. He also maintained that any proposal to use loans rather than taxes, if it were to follow his rule, required the removal of any "debt illusion" because the manner of debt servicing had to be voted on at the same time. In fact, Wicksell was strongly in favour of a fairly rigid balance budget requirement.[1]

However, the development of a procedure by which the utility calculus of those representing taxpayers in Parliament could be more effectively operated was not enough for Wicksell. To produce an analogue to the pricing system for private goods required that the decision rule should approximate the result of unanimous consent. Ruling out unanimous consent "for practical reasons"[2] Wicksell settled for a decision rule based on qualified majority. For voting on the continuance of previously existing obligations (such as interest and amortisation payments on the public debt) he accepted that a simple majority rule would be sufficient, but for the bulk of budget decisions, whether involving new expenditure and new taxes or changes in the composition of taxes and expenditure, the required qualified majority would have to be at least three-fourths.

It is worth noting that Wicksell was seeking a solution to the problem posed by de Tocqueville arising from the extension of the franchise and to which the Classical economists could only offer the solution of "hastening slowly" in that extension until the "lower classes" had a property stake.[3] Wicksell, however, accepted universal suffrage in principle but echoed de Tocqueville's prediction:

[if] once the lower classes are definitely in possession of the power to legislate and tax, there will certainly be a danger that they may behave no more unselfishly than those classes which have so far been in power. In other words, there will be danger that the lower classes in power may impose the bulk of all taxes on the rich and may at the same time be so reckless and extravagant in approving public expenditures to which they themselves contribute but little that the nation's mobile capital may soon be squandered fruitlessly. This may

1. *Ibid.*, p. 91.
2. *Ibid.*, p. 92.
3. See the Third Lecture.

well break the lever of progress. This danger should not be dismissed lightly nor belittled especially not by those who feel, as I do, that the advance of democracy is so rightful an end.

And then he adds:

[there] can be no doubt that the best and indeed the only certain guarantee against such abuses of power lies in the principle of unanimity and voluntary consent in the approval of taxes.[1]

The number of references to Wicksell's ideas in the modern literature on public goods is legion but what is interesting is how, over the last thirty years, there has been a change in attitude towards their inspirational content. The "Wicksellian Perspective", as it has been labelled by Tollison and Wagner,[2] initially provided a solution to a problem in welfare economics posed by the impossibility of pricing public goods, and which rejected the device of the "ethical observer" who would read our minds on our preferences and "realise" our wishes by compulsion. Wicksell's posthumous imprimatur was sought in order to legitimise the contractarian approach to fiscal politics. Today, his principle of approximate unanimity is additionally invoked in order to prevent a bias against "excessive" public expenditure that would result from simple majority rule. That rule reduces the tax/price to the majority who can shift part of the cost of expenditure that they favour onto the minority, which enables a majority to support larger budgets than they would choose if its members had to bear their full cost.

The first problem presented by the Wicksellian fiscal reforms is how to engineer a constitutional change when faced with the "hall of mirrors" paradox.[3] Would it be realistic to suppose, or indeed legitimate, that the constitutional change would be instituted by a legislature which had bound itself by a simple majority rule? Say the legislature was open to motions which proposed alternative voting rules, which voting rule would be

1. WICKSELL, 'A New Principle of Just Taxation', *op. cit.*, p. 95.
2. ROBERT D. TOLLISON and RICHARD E. WAGNER, 'Balanced Budgets and Beyond', in BUCHANAN, ROWLEY and TOLLISON, eds., *Deficits, op. cit.*, p. 385.
3. See the laconic criticism of Wicksell by IAIN MACLEAN, *Dealing in Votes*, Oxford: Martin Robertson, 1982, p. 158 and footnote 1, p. 194.

acceptable in order to decide which voting rule motion should be adopted – and so on ad infinitum? Wicksell does make it clear in his Preface to *Finanztheoretische Untersuchungen* that he is not concerned with practical implementation of any of his proposals:

I am ready to admit that much of my discussion may be classified as armchair speculation. I accept the title gladly, for this is, in fact, the manner in which evertything may be taken into account, and an inclusive, internally consistent system constructed. For this reason, I never worry about the external consequences of carrying out my theory. How much of it – or whether any at all – may be practically applied in the near future, practical men may decide. I become the same as they if I try to take into account every conceivable practical criticism.

It is significant that this passage prefaces James Buchanan's *Public Finance in Democratic Process*.[1] Wicksell was an optimist about social progress and wrote when representative government and the form it might take in his own country was still in process of evolution. Radical ideas might still take root, particularly if, as Wicksell found in later life, he was more disposed not to follow his own maxim of confining his activities to "armchair speculation".[2] So far as the "hall of mirrors" problem is concerned, how constitutional change designed to check the power of strong vested interests is to be instituted is not on the agenda of contractarian public choice analysts. They must be putting their money on the Keynesian supposition that ideas will triumph in the end. However, their own description of how men behave when faced with economic and political choices does not lead me to assign a high probability to the chances of their immediate success, even if one wishes it were otherwise.

Let it be assumed, however, that a qualified majority rule is passed and embodied in the fiscal clauses of the Constitution. Would this be sufficient to achieve the end of limiting the growth in *G/GDP*?

---

1. *Op. cit.*, p. 2.
2. For the evidence, see CARL G. UHR, *The Economic Doctrines of Knut Wicksell*, Berkeley and Los Angeles: University of California Press, 1962, Chapters 1 and 12.

In a remarkable essay on Wicksell's principles, Black shows, by an application of his own voting theory, that, assuming single-peaked preferences for all members of the legislature, Wicksell's procedures would introduce a highly effective barrier against increasing state expenditure.[1] This is because Wicksell's qualified majority would require a high majority in order to give effect to an increase in expenditure, whereas a small minority would be sufficient to engineer a reduction.[2] It is certainly not clear that Wicksell realised this. He certainly maintained that his rules would curb irresponsible fiscal behaviour but at one point he predicts that

[if] the distribution of taxes always rested on voluntary consent, it seems to me highly probable that many such activities which today can be undertaken only by private groups, would come to be incorporated in the operation of the state.[3]

His own views of the role of the state put considerable emphasis on the state's role in the formation of human capital and on protection against risks of old age, unemployment, accident and ill health; in other words he was a supporter of the welfare state. Apart from the interesting fact that these views hardly accord with those of many contractarians who have derived inspiration from his analytical work, how could they be made compatible with his fiscal rules? Here one can only speculate for his views on the state's role were developed at length some time after his

1. DUNCAN BLACK, 'Wicksell's Principle in the Distribution of Taxation', in *Economic Essays in Commemoration of the Dundee School of Economics, 1931-1955*, Dundee, 1955.

2. This is because Wicksell foresaw a difficulty when a reduction in expenditures and revenues is involved because the individual items of revenue and expenditure did not correspond in modern budgets. He offered the solution that each single expenditure category should be assigned to a particular revenue category, the relevant decision about assignment being decided by simple majority. Having done this, he proposed that only a fraction of the legislature (up to 25 per cent of its members) should be able to demand removal of any tax category, implying an associated reduction in expenditure. This would leave the legislature with the option of altering the tax distribution or to agreeing to the abolition or reduction of the appropriate expenditure. See WICKSELL, 'A New Principle of Just Taxation', *op. cit.*, p. 94.

3. *Ibid.*, p. 89.

views on the rules themselves. His biographer, Carl Uhr,[1] indicates two explanations. The first is that Wicksell envisaged a shift in tastes and preferences of voters away from military expenditures towards social expenditures as the franchise was extended to the working classes. The second is that investment in human capital would contribute so effectively towards increasing *GDP* that the *G/GDP* ratio would not increase.

Returning to the present day, you will note that much depends on which explanations of the growth of public expenditure are considered to be quantitatively significant. Those who emphasise that supply factors play an important if not a decisive role in that growth are bound to argue that constitutional rules are primarily designed to prevent interest groups on the demand side from exploiting their position and will remain unconvinced. Well-established government departments with a monopoly of information on the cost of providing government services and in a position to claim that productivity gains are less likely to occur in the public sector,[2] may be able to protect Leviathan from the new pressures for economy derived from constitutional reform. An overall limitation on the aggregate size and growth of the public budget would need to be added to the list of constitutional provisions.[3]

Indeed, I would argue that some such provision would be necessary in order to give proper effect to Wicksell's own recommendations. These latter concentrate on the annual budget and on preventing the growth in future tax burdens emanating from the substitution of debt for tax finance. A qualified majority rule is not necessarily a protection against future obligations of the government which are unfunded. The most important example is represented today by state retirement schemes based on a pay-as-you-go system of finance, which have received widespread political support. It is surely in the spirit of Wicksell's

1. See UHR, *The Economic Doctrines of Knut Wicksell, op. cit.*, Chapter 12, *passim*.
2. As already argued in the Second Lecture.
3. This point is recognised by TOLLISON and WAGNER, 'Balanced Budgets and Beyond', *op. cit.*, pp. 384-7. For further discussion of such limitations, see my essay 'Macro-Economic Controls of Spending as a Device for Improving Efficiency in Government', in FORTE and PEACOCK, eds., *Public Expenditure and Government Growth, op. cit.*, pp. 143-68.

reforms that unenfranchised future generations should have some protection, unless present voters' utility functions embody arguments relating to the satisfaction they may derive from not over-burdening their heirs by a commitment to pay for an excessive amount towards their retirement incomes.[1]

1. For further development of such issues, see my essay, 'Is There a Public Debt Problem in Developed Countries?, *op. cit.*

5. Epilogue

Let me recall the very limited nature of my investigations. It was to advance the thesis that in the study of public finance the history of political economy, if not an essential, is certainly a highly desirable input for the further development of its analytical content. It must be emphasised that I have only considered part of the available evidence. The traditional core of public finance, namely the theory of taxation, has not been under scrutiny. It might even be claimed that my case would be better illustrated from a study of the influence of ideas on distributive justice on currently accepted maxims of "optimal" taxation. One notes, for example, that even at the textbook level (though it is much more than an ordinary textbook!) Richard and Peggy Musgrave recommend students to read Bentham, Locke and Marx, alongside Phelps, Rawls and Tobin.[1] Nor would I claim that my selection of "inputs" comprehends all the major figures of the past who might have something to teach us about our present concerns. This is clearly demonstrated in the neglect of Italian writers, and it may strike some of you as rather strange that Amilcare Puviani received "star billing"! I would also be the first to admit that the inspirational content of past writing will fluctuate as the concerns of writers in public finance alter, as they are bound to do.

It would be interesting at the end of these lectures to take a vote on the "motion" that I have proposed. I suspect, however, that an Italian audience would be unrepresentative and that a Wicksellian qualified majority in favour of such a modest motion would not be too difficult to obtain from them. More interesting, perhaps, would be a motion in favour of the proposition that the history of political economy is an essential part of the equipment of a specialist on public finance. I suspect that the division of the vote in this case might depend on whether or not the ballot was secret! But, as I have already indicated, I cannot convince myself that I would support the motion, even though I believe that

1. See their *Public Finance in Theory and Practice*, Fourth edition, New York: McGraw-Hill, 1984, p. 101.

any contribution I may have made to the understanding of public policy questions has been markedly influenced by a study of the Classics.

Despite what I have said about the conspiracy to kill the past to which I made early reference, let me quote from that isolated and remarkable Brito-Spanish economist who still haunts our textbooks and who did not subscribe to contemporary fashion (incidentally, he read French, Spanish, Dutch, Italian and German!):

To trace the affiliation of ideas in the progress of science is calculated to correct our estimates of authority: to reduce in general the extravagant regard which the youthful student is apt to entertain for contemporary leaders, and to assign due weight to real originality.[1]

Justice has certainly been done to Edgeworth who wrote that passage, and it is my hope that it will long continue to be done to writers of his calibre and integrity.

1. FRANCIS Y. EDGEWORTH, 'The Objects and Methods of Political Economy', in *Papers Relating to Political Economy*, London: Macmillan, 1925, vol. 1, p. 11.

COMMENTARIES

FRANCESCO FORTE*

1. Let me first consider the preliminary question dealt with by Sir Alan Peacock: whether the history of economic ideas is an essential part not only of the education but also of the training of an economist, and, what is more, requires professional economists to refer back to it. The masterly treatment by Sir Alan of some of the topical issues of public choice theory in the light of the historical perspective – in the present lectures – should be evidence of its great usefulness.

Let me, however, point out that the methodology followed by him in employing the history of thought to explore theoretical (public choice) issues is very different from that which is commonly considered as the most appropriate in the history of science and therefore – because of the predominant "scientism" – also in economic science. Normally one considers the history of thought as a succession of attempts at approaching the truth, through a process of analytical and empirical improvement, refutation and innovation of knowledge. In this perspective, economists of an earlier period appear as rather naive scholars, whose thought should be merely considered as primitive reasoning to be subsequently replaced by that of their successors. Ideas, in a sense, gradually develop, like a child, from the embryonic to the adult stage, to old age, and finally die. Dead ideas, however, deserve rediscovery because in this way we can understand how the process of expansion of our knowledge took place and because by reviewing the theoretical discoveries of our illustrious predecessors we are expected to learn how to make our own discoveries and to understand and judge scientific progress, while paying the necessary tribute to the glories of our profession.

2. This may be an interesting point of view – and indeed has been developed by such historians of economic thought as Joseph Schumpeter – but it is not the most relevant for us, as

* Professor of Public Finance, Università di Roma «La Sapienza».

theoretical economists and as interdisciplinary scholars. Nor is it the point of view adopted by Sir Alan here.

What he essentially does in providing us with an historical perspective of some of the hottest issues of public choice theory and policy, is to improve our knowledge about them by re-calling important seminal contributions of the past, which have been insufficiently considered. His reflection on them gives us new insights or new perspectives into the assessment of the complexity of the cases. "Classics" are written by those authors who are interesting not simply as prophets but as permanent sources of reference.

In addition, he provides us with important reflections on the connection between the environmental conditions and the chang-ing models of public choice games and their perverse and virtuous results, if any. The historical perspective at the level of thought therefore, if it is to bear fruit, becomes an empirical perspective of the consequences of the varying factual situations.

Thirdly, Sir Alan's historical perspective of public choice aims at inviting us to consider whether long run "laws" which have been formulated in the past, analysing the working of given public choice mechanisms, did really operate or were falsified.

For instance, does present evidence confirm the various laws of public sector growth from Wagner to Puviani, to Peacock and Wiseman, to Buchanan and Wagner, to Niskanen and Baumol and to Bruno Frey?

3. Let me now move to a second general point: the definition of the public choice approach to the analysis of public economics.

From my own point of view the theoretical network of public economics can consist only of the public choice thread. This is so because the axiomatic approach employing a social welfare function given to politicians by some external, "competent" armchair observer on the basis or with the constraint of the ethical values which appear to be the most acceptable or of alternative ethical values suitable to that status and on the basis of his assertion on the utility curves – as Peacock repeatedly notes – is an imperialistic construction to be imposed from the outside on "Pavlovian individuals".

In a sense, Public Economics as a branch of Theoretical Welfare Economics embodying a social welfare function deduced from a set of values and developed through the utility axioms, may be a theory of normative economics, but cannot be a theory of positive economics.

4. On the other hand, a theory of normative economics devoid of a positive economics counterpart rests on two possible options: the first is to assume that the positive side of the problem lies in the jurisdiction of sociology and politics, i.e. is a matter of sociological knowledge, as Pareto forcefully maintained (and certainly his "welfare economics", as noted by Sir Alan, is not the one presently known as Paretian welfare economics).

The second is to let positive economics describe the "effects" on the market economy of the decisions undertaken by the public authority.

Obviously, those effects are viewed only partially, i.e. over-looking the "non-Pavlovian" strategical effects, as Forte and Peacock have argued, particularly in the introductory chapter of their jointly edited book on the *Political Economy of Taxation*.[1]

Thus, while the first option is defective or "desertionist", because it foregoes analysis of an area of economic behaviour which, nowadays, includes nearly half (or more) of the aggregate income of the developed nations, the second is misleading. This is because in the chain of the actions and reactions at the second or third act of the drama, the important variable of the first act and maybe of the second ignore it, and also because only a part of these "outcomes" (i.e. events resulting from other events) are considered and many other influences are overlooked.

5. After this statement of public choice "chauvinism" *vis-à-vis* public economics, let me consider Peacock's definition of the public choice approach to public economics. He says: "Public choice analysis is the examination of individual and group decision making in the conduct of transactions which, while analogous to those of the market, do not replicate market

---

1. Oxford: Blackwell, 1981.

situations, in which the outcome of these decisions will be a set of prices and outputs. It produces hypotheses about the outcome of these transactions."[1]

Sir Alan then identifies the three major political markets in which such an hypothesis can be developed: i.e. the "primary political market in which politicians sell policies for votes", where the theories of voting rules in relation to public expenditure tendencies have been developed; the "policy supply market in which bureaucrats will offer alternative administrative packages" according to choices and behaviour which are now incorporated in the theory of bureaucracy; the "policy execution market", relating to taxpayers and public expenditure beneficiaries who "more or less passively" adjust to the decision of the law and try to influence the law's application through their organized activities, so that "regulators may be captured by the regulated".

The theory of tax avoidance and of tax planning, which Peacock and I tried to develop, enters in this last section of the public choice fiscal process.

Obviously, as Sir Alan stresses, the public choice/political markets domain is wider: it also includes for instance international bargaining where "bargains are struck without exchange of money". It includes bargains between nations about tariffs, ecology, macroeconomic actions and international monetary regulation. It includes negotiations between the Treasury and the Central Bank and those between the Government, public utilities and the citizens involved in them as consumers or as suppliers of factors of production.

The bargains in political markets have different outcomes from those in economic markets not only because of different arguments, but also because they have essentially been manifested by different procedures. The exchange and competitive processes are different from those in private commercial markets. Behaviour in the political or public units of supply of goods and services is not subject to market pressures.

1. See Lecture 1, p. 13.

6. It seems to me that the unifying conceptual framework to analyse the public choices/political markets/political firms problems, is to be found in the emergence of the rules of the game, requiring, therefore, the use of game-theoretical modelling of behaviour.

This idea developed in my mind gradually, as an outcome of my joint work with Peacock, when we agreed, against the axiomatic views of the current optimal taxation theory, of the current theory of optimality in the area of public spending and of public budgeting, as derived from a social welfare function and/or from neo-Keynesian approaches to macroeconomic equilibrium.

We have repeatedly claimed that one should consider individuals as reacting not as Pavlovian dogs but through strategical behaviour. We have therefore concluded that one should consider the different bargaining situations of the different kinds of taxpayers and bureaucrats faced with different kinds of measures. We were often in search of rules which would assure an equilibrium which may occur in real life, and not one devised at armchair level. We sought some form of workable, not imaginary, justice.

What do these concepts or propositions of a game-theory character consist of? Different rules of the game produce different results. The imposition of equilibrium solutions which are also saddle points from a game theory point of view may provide reasonably stable solutions.

To illustrate the enormous potentiality of application of the game-theory conceptual tools to the public choice approach, let me take the concept of "tax avoidance" which has been worked out by Sir Alan and subsequently applied in our joint work on tax theory, from a "strategic" (or game strategic, as I would like to say now) point of view. Tax avoidance includes both tax evasion and escape from taxation through legal but unfair means and may also include straight escape from taxation through legal and fair means, such as transferring one's real domicile to a different city or region or nation which provides better public services at lower tax costs.

There is a clear-cut game-theory distinction between unfair tax avoidance and fair tax avoidance: the first consists in free ride behaviour, through which one defects from the (not easily enforceable) rules of the game; the second consists of simple desertion from the game.

Let me say that Sir Alan's thought, which has been important for me in developing this point of view, has been stimulated by also finding a point of reference in the history of ideas of public choice.

De Viti de Marco's and Einaudi's, and Mazzola's "laws" and "economics of public finance", i.e. the "economic laws" of the Italian tradition of *economia finanziaria*, when carefully analysed, are a mixture between concepts of equilibrium in public economy and concepts of optimality, where the two points of view may be reconciled in the game-theory frame of search for optimal equilibrium solutions of the public economy or public choice games.

7. Peacock has been too modest in presenting his own contribution to the development of the public choice approach to public economics.

My specific comments on his four Lectures will be mostly devoted to pinpointing these contributions. Needless to say the main school of public choice is that known as the Virginia Public Choice School, tracing back to the Nobel Laureate James Buchanan who now heads it at the James Mason University and to Gordon Tullock, the editor of the journal, *Public Choice*, and author of innumerable contributions together with and separately from James Buchanan.

But there are also increasingly important European streams of public choice thought. And I believe that the Peacock School – if I may use this expression for his writing, teaching and co-authoring – has provided fruitful contributions and continuously provides new ones. Aside from the far from trivial reason of mentioning the present European scholars – and actually Bruno Frey as leader of the German School should also be recalled in this context so as not to give the impression that public choice is (only) made in the United States – there is a more specific reason to consider Peacock's contributions to the subject, i.e. that they often have policy implications with a different flavour.

In other words, public choice theory is broader, in its scope, than the public choice policy suggestions of James Buchanan or of Buchanan and Tullock or of Tullock or of Buchanan and Wagner or of Buchanan and Brennan.

Peacock's book with Charles K. Rowley, *Welfare Economics: A Liberal Restatement*,[1] written nearly fifteen years ago, as he says, in his First Lecture "emphasiz[es] the liberal rejection of the view that all outcomes of democratic voting rules are necessarily desirable, though that does not mean that a liberal need reject the liberal voting rules themselves".[2] Sir Alan is too modest in this quotation from himself. Actually in the book there is the most persuasive and philosophically broad contribution to the theory of the "impossibility of the Paretian liberal", developed and defended with endless vigour by Amartya Sen. Paretian welfare economics, Rowley and Peacock demonstrate, may lead to so-called welfare optima which, from the liberal point of view, are inconsistent with the optimum.

In other words, accepting given values which one may define as the "Liberal principle", a solution, deriving from general agreement of the (considered) voters, which – by definition, satisfies the principle of the Paretian optimum since it makes somebody better off in terms of his or her preferences while nobody is worse off – does not need to satisfy the liberal principle. The Sen theory, Peacock and Rowley argue, is not decisive for demonstrating the "impossibility": because the "L" condition of Sen is much less than the liberal requisite and because lexicographic ordering of ethical values is rarely relevant in the real world and there exists a problem of conflicts of freedom on which a degree of coercion, according to the liberal postulates, is necessary. It would take us too far here to try to summarize Peacock and Rowley's analysis both of the rejection of Sen's particular (first) demonstration of his theory and of the position through which he set forth the contrast between Paretianism (in the neo-Paretian sense) and "true" liberalism. I would, however, like to underline that this is not only a kind of philosophical-

1. CHARLES K. ROWLEY and ALAN T. PEACOCK, *Welfare Economics: A Liberal Restatement*, London: Martin Robertson, 1975.
2. See above, p. 16.

methodological attack; it is also a manifold public choice analysis of the collective decision-making game having to do with the various kinds of freedom of the various classes of subjects, be they individuals or organised groups.

Furthermore "It is true to say that liberals with other individuals obtain positive utility from economic advances, but where these are in conflict with important negative freedoms, they personally would discount the economic benefits more sharply than would Paretian liberals, i.e. they attach a higher value to freedom".[1]

That public choice analysis of the liberal principle could be developed fruitfully from these ground-breaking outlines, seems to me at once obvious and desirable so as to promote a courageous exploration of these largely untouched areas of conflicts of values, as driving forces of collective organization.

8. Peacock's Second Lecture is basically devoted to the discussion of the voting issues in the light of the de Tocqueville median voter theory and of the theories derived therefrom about public expenditure growth. Here I would like to draw attention to the original contribution of Sir Alan through his "de Tocqueville Cross". The Buchanan and Tullock voting rule (basically a qualified majority rule) is derived from the confrontation between the (high) exploitation costs deriving from a narrow majority rule and the (high) transaction costs deriving from a (close to) unanimity rule. Examining Peacock's de Tocqueville Cross one may sort out a qualified majority rule on the basis of the type of income distribution which appears to be present in the society considered and of the subsequent "dangers" of "populist" income redistribution which maybe emanated through the de Tocqueville Paradox. On the other hand, the "cross" relates incomes and taxes on these, which are assumed to be either proportional or progressive as measured on incomes. For a tax system where (nearly) constitutional limits exist to the height of the marginal rates and to the taxation of minimum incomes, this relation may change: median voters may still have incomes

1. Rowley and Peacock, *Welfare Economics, op. cit.,* p. 90.

124

slightly below the "average", but it may well be that in the case of a general tax increase, they would bear an "average" burden, because those with higher incomes and greater wealth are hardly taxable on their revenues at a proportional rate, while those at the lowest income level cannot be reached by taxation.

Observing the de Tocqueville Cross, for a given country with these more specific relations, it may well be that the trend towards the "irrational" increase of public spending cannot be explained through the de Toqueville Paradox, but calls for other explanations.

And actually Peacock in this very lecture offers two of the most important contributions, still related to the franchise of voting.

Firstly, "if the proportion of G (government expenditure) financed by borrowing increases and if governments issue interest-bearing debt to the private sector, then interest payments to present generations of taxpayers/voters may make the pre-tax distribution of income more unequal and at the same time may encourage the relatively rich to substitute investment income for labour income. The translation of these complicated distributional and incentive effects into a demand for G becomes much more complicated".[1]

Secondly, there is the "intergeneration" bargain problem as Sir Alan – with a game-theory terminology – describes the issue of burden on contributors and taxpayers of future generations in favour of present voters – through better retirement schemes paid by the social security institutions.

Whatever can be said about Barro's Ricardian theory of equivalence, it should be clear that – up to now – this is a "concealed debt" and, therefore, cannot enter the paradigm of changes of behaviour of present citizens/savers in the way which Barro claims new public debt would cause. On the contrary, it enters on the appropriate side of the account, since future pensioners need to save less to maintain their income in old age, if their perspectives of pensions are improved.

The implications of this seminal contribution of Peacock to

1. See Lecture 2, p. 52.

the issues of the intergenerational public choice game have not yet been fully appreciated.

9. There is a way, obviously, to reconcile the de Tocqueville paradigm with the isolation paradox paradigm of irrational growth of public spending just described: that there is a request by less than median voters, to get individual goods free of charge or at a very low price from the public sector, to improve their real income. But perhaps at this point one should also consider the rent seeking activity by the various interest groups.

10. The Third Lecture is mostly devoted to the issues of the theory of bureaucracy, one of the areas of public economics opened up by the public choice approach. Peacock's contribution to this subject is particularly important. In his words, it consists in developing a variant of the economic analysis of bureaucracy which can serve as a suitable framework of analysis for the procedures associated with attempts to remove X-inefficiency. In placing emphasis on what has been called the "entrenched lethargy"[1] of bureaucrats, the analysis embodies a characteristic of such beings by the Classical economists and their descendants. It is believed that this additional dimension to the analysis directs attention towards a neglected feature of bureaucratic supply, namely regulation of the "market between bureaus".

Sir Alan analyses the prospects of removal of X-inefficiency by comparison between antimonopoly investigation in the private, as contrasted with the public sector.[2]

But, perhaps, the most important inference from Sir Alan's analysis is that "competition" among public bureaus should be promoted as a remedy to their X-inefficiency and as a basis for monitoring this inefficiency.

11. The Fourth Lecture is devoted to the theme of the constitutional limits to the Leviathan: in my terminology, to the

---

1. See LESLIE CHAPMAN, *Your Disobedient Servant*, London: Chatto and Windus, 1978.
2. See Lecture 4, pp. 88-9.

proper rules of the public choice game, to get results which are rational from a game theory point of view.

The issue is very broad and my remaining time very short. I will therefore only mention two points of Peacock's analysis, relating to his valuable contributions to the subject.

The first has to do with the fact that since future generations do not participate in the public choice game now, it is not enough to require a qualified majority to avoid "irrational" public spending growth. It is necessary to introduce limitations on the size and growth of the public budget.

The second has to do with the issues of fiscal illusion. This theme which traces back to Puviani's contribution has received little attention in the literature on fiscal constitution.

Perhaps the reason is that – as Sir Alan points out – Puviani's book is referred to, by English-speaking (or German-speaking, English-reading) scholars, mostly by hearsay, since no translation has been published.

Yet, as shown in a theoretical contribution by Anibal Cavaco-Silva, one of the most prominent members of the Peacock School, and by Emilio Giardina, this may be a very important point in influencing public spending financed through deficits.

I would take as one of the most interesting fruits of Peacock's Mattioli Lectures the reflection on changes in behaviour of citizens and their representatives, as possible constituents resulting from full information on perverse changes in distribution of income, on unemployment and on the reduction of balanced economic growth resulting from a large public debt and from the modest legacy of additional collective or private capital which the huge deficit in our country has produced.

BRUNO S. FREY*

1. Introduction

Political Economy or Public Choice is an important area in which great progress has been achieved and important insights have been gained. It is not part of conventional economics but is by most economists seen as an aspect which may be taken into account if one likes – but which one can disregard without any problem at all. I therefore greatly welcome Professor Peacock's Mattioli Lectures, and I would like to congratulate the organizers on having chosen Sir Alan, one of the most influential and prolific researchers in political economy.

It goes without saying that I greatly enjoyed the Mattioli Lectures. I personally am convinced that the views proffered by Professor Peacock cannot be overestimated, views which are based on a broad perspective of the issues, a concentration on relevant problems, combined with a clear reasoning. This approach compares favourably with much of current economics, and I am sorry to say, also part of Public Choice, which tends to be reduced to some kind of applied mathematics.

I should like to concentrate my remarks on two aspects: the message of Political Economy, and the role and use of the History of Economic Thought.

2. The Message of Political Economy

a. Political fails: In Political Economy (a term which I prefer to the rather narrow concept of "Public Choice") it is generally accepted that political processes do not function perfectly. Rather, all decision-making mechanisms "fail", i.e. they have shortcomings which prevent them from functioning optimally or even efficiently. It has been shown by Political Economists that democratic procedures do not necessarily lead to social welfare maximization (however defined) but that they may

* Professor of Economics, University of Zurich.

lead to contradictory and irrational results. The failure of decision making by bureaucracies and by bargaining among interest groups has also been the subject of analysis, and has been
stressed in Professor Peacock's lectures.

The study of the "failure of politics" undertaken in Political
Economy has been a reaction to "market failure" as proposed by
welfare economics in the 1960s. At that time (and some economists still believe in that view) it was generally accepted that when
market failure exists, government intervention is automatically
needed. For political economists it is, in contrast, clear that this
conclusion is unwarranted, and that a comparative evaluation
of the workings of the various decision-making systems is needed.

In much of (American) Public Choice a further conclusion
has been reached: it is argued that markets are generally
superior, and that politics is almost always inferior. However,
this conclusion is based more on an ideological presupposition
than on analysis, and it certainly does not follow from Political
Economy.

b. The real message: In Sir Alan's lectures the value of democracy
in comparison with an authoritarian system has been treated more
implicitly than explicitly. Democracy can, and should, be looked
at as that decision-making procedure taking individual preferences
into account, or enabling the orderly change between parties in
power according to election results. Analysing these aspects in
depth, Political Economy has provided new and relevant insights which compare most favourably with the naive view of
orthodox economics which assumes either that no government
exists, or that governments automatically maximize social welfare quite irrespective of their form. It is indeed assumed that the
government behaves in the same way whether it is a dictatorship
or a democracy.

What matters is not the juxtaposition of market failure with
political failure but to compare democratic with authoritarian
decisions. In his lectures, Sir Alan refers to Lord Keynes'
"Harvey Road mentality", the view that the cognoscenti or the
intellectual aristocracy should and must tell people what has
to be done. This view corresponds at best to a benevolent

dictatorship, but in most cases turns out to be far from benevolent. The real message of Political Economy thus has to do with the virtues of democracy compared to other political decision-making systems.

c. The dangers of authoritarianism: It could be argued that the emphasis on the virtues of democracy here postulated are of little relevance because we fortunately live in democracies, and authoritarianism is no real danger. However, I would like to submit that there is always the danger of lapsing into this direction. Indeed, it may often be observed in our democracies that solutions to social problems are sought by resorting to dictatorial measures, disregarding democratic procedures and individual preferences.

An example is the modern ecological movement which is of considerable importance today in Germany and Scandinavia, and which has recently gained momentum in France, and is predictably important also in Italy. Many of the "Greens" have a marked tendency to deal with environmental problems by applying draconian measures. Environmental policy is solely seen in terms of prohibitions, and those damaging nature must be harshly punished. Those not agreeing with this policy tend to be considered criminals, to be treated as outcasts losing their human and political rights.

Political Economy shows convincingly that this approach implies two major mistakes. The first is that a disregard for preferences of some parts of the population leads to a resistance to the well-meant policies undertaken. As a result, the policies have only partial effect. The second mistake is that a reliance on prohibitions necessarily requires the intensive use of public bureaucracy. Public officials, however, pursue their own ends, thus diverting from the intended goals.

3. The Role and Use of the History of Economic Thought

a. Its usefulness: Sir Alan has persuasively argued that the history of economic doctrines is of great use for understanding political economy, and the economy in general. (But he also pointed out that there are opportunity costs involved.) He concludes that a knowledge of our past economic masters' thinking is a necessary but not a sufficient condition for good economics.

b. Is it in fact useful?: I would like to take a somewhat different view. The problem is not that there are no important ideas with former economists, rather the contrary is true: there are few ideas which could not in some form or other be detected in the writings of the classics.

The problem is that these ideas cannot be seen, or grasped, in the writings of the dead masters, without having the idea *beforehand*. What happens in effect is that the ideas and theories are looked up in the past writings only after such ideas have been discussed in modern analysis. It is often an *ex post* exercise, a kind of make-up, which not rarely serves solely the purpose of exhibiting one's erudition.

To support the proposition that the history of economic thought is mainly of *ex post* use, three areas may be mentioned:

(i) *Social accounting*: As is well known, this analysis was developed by Richard Stone and James Meade in Britain in order to better evaluate the resource constraints of the Second World War effort. Only later was it discovered that at the end of the seventeenth century Gregory King was engaged in the same endeavour, including a prediction of how long it is possible to pursue a particular war.

(ii) *Preference aggregation*: In the early 1950s Kenneth Arrow proved that no aggregation of individual preferences meeting reasonable and democratic conditions is generally possible without risking logical inconsistency.[1] This study has had great impact on economics, and has brought to light a new area of enquiry, social choice. It became known only later, mainly through the works of Duncan Black,[2] that there are many precursors to Arrow's

---

1. KENNETH J. ARROW, *Social Choice and Individual Values*, New Haven: Yale University Press, 1951 (Second edition, 1963).
2. DUNCAN BLACK, *The Theory of Committees and Elections*, Cambridge: Cambridge University Press, 1971.

findings. Indeed, scholars like Lewis Carroll (the Reverend Dodgson, student of Christ Church, Oxford, and author of *Alice in Wonderland*) have extensively written about the preference aggregation paradox, and have even applied it to practical problems.

(iii) *Party competition*: One of the most influential books in Modern Political Economy has been Anthony Downs' *Economic Theory of Democracy*, published in 1957.[1] No reference was made by him, nor by the writers following him, to Joseph Schumpeter who in his *Capitalism, Socialism and Democracy*, published in 1942,[2] very clearly discussed party competition. Indeed, in many respects, Schumpeter went further than Downs. Nevertheless, nobody engaged in the early efforts to develop party competition theory in early Public Choice remembered this important forerunner. This is all the more surprising because Schumpeter was in his time, and is still today, one of the most famous economists.

How can this incapacity to take up the relevant ideas in the works of the past masters at the right time be explained? I should like to suggest that there may be two quite different kinds of knowledge contained in the writings of the past. The first type of knowledge is perceived, and there is no problem to retrieve it. The second type of knowledge cannot be put to use because it is outside one's consideration or outside one's *ipsative possibility set*.[3]

4. Consequences

What are the conclusions to be drawn for the teaching of the history of doctrines to students of economics? Based on what has been said above, two possibilities suggest themselves:

1. ANTHONY DOWNS, *An Economic Theory of Democracy*, New York: Harper and Row, 1957.

2. JOSEPH A. SCHUMPETER, *Capitalism, Socialism and Democracy*, New York: Harper, 1942.

3. See, for a discussion of this concept, BRUNO S. FREY, 'Ipsative and Objective Limits to Human Behaviour', *Journal of Behavioral Economics*, Winter 1988, pp. 229-48.

(i) Students could be taught to actively exploit the ideas contained in the writings of the past masters. This solution is not attractive because it means that history is used instrumentally, only. More importantly, it does not appear to be feasible after what has been said above: if one does not have an idea beforehand, one does not know what to look for in the past literature.

(ii) The second solution is to leave the situation as it is today, i.e. not to expose students – and in particular beginners – to any special training in the history of economic thought. This solution is based on the notion that the history of economic ideas is such a fascinating and beautiful topic that only those people should study it who do it voluntarily and on their own initiative; but no student should be *forced* to engage in it. It is too valuable a subject to be imposed upon people who might resent it (partly due to the opportunity costs mentioned). Rather, the history of economic doctrines should be reserved for accomplished and cultured scholars who do not only love it but also put it to good use. In his Mattioli Lectures Sir Alan has given us a delightful example of such an undertaking.

EMILIO GERELLI*

1. First of all let me say that after reading Professor Peacock's papers I feel as relaxed as one can be after a successful psychoanalytic session. I refer here particularly to that part of his papers where he expounds the links between the history of economic ideas and the equipment of a professional economist. In my young days, in fact, I was told, as was Professor Peacock, that "there were positive dangers perceived in concentrating on the scholastic aspects of the history of ideas" since scholasticism was seen as "a poor substitute for evidence of analytical ability".[1] For a certain time, by and large, I followed this advice, and although I later steered a middle course between analysis and scholasticism, I somewhat always felt a bit guilty for not having devoted more time of my early years to the "classics". As I said at the outset I feel now relieved by the fact that according to Alan Peacock's lectures (which I truly enjoyed both for the author's constructive capacity and his culture) my original sin may not doom me to hell after all.

For this reason, I shall go on sinning happily by applying here as well Professor Peacock's provocative statement contained in his 1957 Inaugural Lecture to the effect that his period of reference with regard to economic doctrine was "the next ten years and beyond".[2]

2. Professor Peacock's main theme is public choice and the growth of public expenditures. I do not want to make unnecessary compliments in the old Spanish tradition which has been mastered by my countrymen very well, but I must still say that any attempt to innovate with regard to Professor Peacock's authoritative contribution would amount to succumb to the general law according to which *nihil sub sole novi*. I shall however try to find a way out by considering the impact on public expenditures

* Professor of Public Finance, Università di Pavia.
1. See Lecture 1, pp. 5, 6.
2. *Ibid.*, p. 5.

of particular technological breakthroughs which entail social decision about human life. Public choice analysis is a useful tool to help understand the increasingly important problems just mentioned.

3. The scenario I want to present is as follows.

Society has always had to decide about human life. The paramount example of such a decision is, of course, whether or not to wage a war. However, before the present century the variety of such decisions was relatively limited. Premature death, earthquakes, floods, typhoons and the like were – and still are – considered as "acts of God" which one must put up with and for which only passive protection of life is possible. One cannot cast a vote on the acceptance of a hurricane.

Of course, medicine has always been a tool for the protection of life. But, before the coming of the Welfare State, social decisions had scarcely anything to do with it, since medicine was considered a private good. Its positive external effects were not taken into consideration. (In fact the rather doubtful effects of medicine in the past centuries amply justify for our eyes the appropriateness of past *laissez-faire* policy, which it would perhaps be useful to reconsider – in my personal opinion – in view of some problematic aspects and the excesses of the modern medical arts.)

The picture, however, is decidedly different nowadays. The rapid introduction of new technologies has surely improved the so-called "quality of life" and reduced certain everyday risks (for instance those deriving from contagious diseases, food poisoning, etc.); at the same time these very technologies are introducing new kinds of risks. Some of them are clear-cut, e.g. car accidents kill about 8,000 people each year in this country (and about 50,000 in the US); major industrial accidents (defined as those causing either more than 50 deaths at a time or more than 100 wounded or a damage of more than 50 million 1987 US dollars) have been 76 in the world (excluding dyke accidents) in the 14 years between 1974 and 1987 and they are growing exponentially since 1920.

Some other categories of new risks, on the contrary, are subtle and difficult to quantify – for instance those connected to the use of medicines and pesticides.

Each of these risks entails both an individual and a social choice. Take the risks associated with driving a car, where one would think at first that the risk of accidents would exclusively depend on personal choices about driving styles, maintenance expenditures, etc. In reality the number of people killed by the car is very much determined by social choices about road design, regulations on car safety (e.g. seat belts) etc. "Thus we comfort ourselves in the belief that our society does not establish an acceptable number of auto deaths, but that this figure results from thousands of independent, atomistic actions."[1]

To conclude on this point, our modern world is characterised by increasing technological risks the level of which very much depends on social choices concerning the amount of resources devoted to avoid or reduce such risks. Such resources may be coming directly from the public budget (e.g. expenditures for better road safety) or determined by government regulations (e.g. higher construction costs for safer cars).

In all such cases the central (though often hidden) issue is the social value given to the life of individuals. It is a very thorny issue for the society because this valuation entails a conflict of values for which there is no easy "rational" solution.

4. Our purpose here is to give a contribution to the analysis of the decision-making mechanisms which are put at work for this type of choices.

We shall not deal here with the "easy" case of social decision-making with regard to the preservation of "statistical lives", which refers to a marginal change in mortality statistics. In such a case, in fact, a rational decision process based on economic calculus would be possible, at least in principle. We shall concern ourselves with the increasing number of cases where the question is not only how to preserve life but how to deal with anxiety and terror (e.g. with regard to nuclear energy and certain developments of biotechnology).

1. GUIDO CALABRESI and PHILIP BOBBITT, *Tragic Choices*, New York: Norton, 1978.

For decision making the difference between the value assigned to the risk of death per se and anxiety (or the fear of death) is relevant. In fact, if we were to ask, for instance, what is worth avoiding the calamity of a major nuclear accident, we would discover that we are concerned both with the anxiety attached to the risk and the low probability event itself. In such cases a rational calculation of the risks and of resources to be devoted to avoid these risks may be hardly relevant.

A seminal contribution to understand how society goes through these conflicting cases is the Theory of Tragic Choices elaborated by the Yale law professor Guido Calabresi.[1] The starting point is the conflict between society's wish, or illusion, to give life an infinite value and the hard fact that this is impossible in a world of scarce resources. To quote: "Tragic choices come about in this way. Though scarcity can often be avoided for some goods by making them available [through public intervention] without cost to everyone, it cannot be evaded for all goods. In the distribution of scarce goods society has to decide which method of allotment to use, and of course each of these methods – markets, political allocations, lotteries and so forth – may be modified or combined with another. The distribution of some goods entails great suffering or death. When attention is riveted on such distributions they arouse emotions of compassion, outrage and terror. It is then that conflicts are laid bare between, on the one hand, those values by which societies determined the beneficiaries of the distributions [e.g. the receivers of hearts for transplant], and (with nature) the perimeters of scarcity, and on the other hand, those humanistic moral values which prize life and well-being".[2]

5. Because of the conflict of ethical values underlying tragic choices no allocation method is fully satisfactory.

Pure markets would blatantly give a money value to human life (e.g. hearts for transplant would be given to those who pay more), which society does not bear to admit openly. Furthermore, certain social objectives would not be taken into account.

1. CALABRESI and BOBBITT, *Tragic Choices, op. cit.*
2. *Ibid.*, p. 18, square brackets ours.

Among the shortcomings of direct regulation, of particular relevance in the case of public choices is the fact that regulation cannot assure a uniform and good quality of decisions, which is required when life is at stake. This happens especially when decisions are numerous and decentralised, e.g. for such bodies as the "ethical committees" in Italy which make decisions about experimenting with new therapies in hospitals.

In other cases (for example when people are sent through the draft to die to the battlefront in traditional wars), a third approach is used. This is decision making through the lottery which is a choice not to choose. A strict equalitarian criterion is thus applied, which is however inconsistent with other principles, such as the principle that "everybody must receive according to his needs".

The last method would not sound new to the readers of Amilcare Puviani's fiscal illusion. "This is less an approach in the manner of the preceding three than an attitude which may be given effect by any of the other methods, or their combination. The attitude consists of the avoidance of self-conscious choice. The method of choosing is not explicitly chosen and may not even be known by the mass of the people. The actual allocations evolve in the society without an explicit selection."[1] The method often used is the moral suasion which is applied nowadays for instance to birth control, and, especially in the past, when patriotic feelings were popular, to allocate the military service.

This method avoids short run political costs, but it runs the risk of blurring the values that the society attributes to decision making, particularly honesty and transparency.

6. All the above four "pure" allocation methods, and also their combinations, are thus less than satisfactory. This happens because when dealing with tragic choices, more than in other cases, we are forced to eschew the assumption that, in resource allocation, efficiency is "the" criterion. We are forced to take account of other conflicting values which are sometimes but a

---

1. *Ibid.*, pp. 44-5.

subterfuge or an illusion, such as the "infinite" value of life. There is thus no optimal solution to a tragic choice, but a mere dwindling from one solution which is consistent with certain values and inconsistent with others to another solution where the situation is changed or reversed.

To quote again: "By complex mixtures of approaches, various societies attempt to avert tragic results, that is, results which imply the rejection of values which are proclaimed to be fundamental. These may succeed for a time. But it will become apparent that some sacrifice of values has taken place; fresh mixtures of methods will be tried, structured ... by the shortcomings of the approaches they replace ... When we have observed this recurrence and continuity of tragedy, it becomes apparent that a special type of mixture is being used by societies over time, namely the mixture or alternation of mixtures. Such a strategy of successive moves comprises an intricate game which better than any other method or set of methods reflects appreciation of the tragic choice.

"It is the most subtle of methods because it depends on methodology being constantly replaced; yet alone among mixtures and methods, cycle strategy does not depend, for its success, on subterfuge. It may represent a forthright way of facing tragic choices since it accepts the fact that society faces the paradox of being forced to choose among competing values in a general context in which none can, for long, be abandoned."[1]

7. Since I am convinced of the appropriateness of the cycle strategy interpretation mentioned above, I believe that a further improvement in the understanding of resource allocation for tragic choices and of the impact of such choices on the size and structure of the public sector could be reached by marrying, as it were, the Theory of Tragic Choices with the Theory of Public Choice. Because of the time limitation, in reality this may not amount to a formal "wedding", but just to an engagement, or perhaps only a date, to examine whether the two offshoots

1. *Ibid.*, pp. 195-6.

match satisfactorily. Perhaps after my attempt others or myself will want to proceed further.

By using the analytical framework of the by now traditional Public Choice paradigm, we propose here to examine the behaviour of the most relevant actors confronted with a tragic choice (i.e. to repeat, a choice strongly characterised by a conflict of ethical values). If we were to list the cast of characters in the order in which they generally (though by no means always) appear on the stage of decision making, the actors are first of all the lobbies which favour, for instance, the introduction of technologies bearing a risk for human life, then the bureaucrats, the politicians and the voters.

In general terms we believe it is easy to accept that the choice about a given issue is more expensive in the case where such a choice is tragic than if the same matter would be considered non-tragic.

In a first approximation our contention is that Calabresi's strategy of cycles would find stabilising forces with two types of actors, the technological-industrial lobby and the voter. However, since each actor promotes a different kind of stability, paradoxically the result would be even greater instability. The strategy of the other two groups of actors, the bureaucrats and the politicians, would, on the contrary, forthrightly (though not openly) favour instability in decision making. Thus, if we introduce our last actor, i.e. the over-burdened tax-payer (considering him for the moment separate from the voter), we would add that his strategy would be to transform as much as possible the tragic choice into a non-tragic choice.

8. Let us now proceed to find some support (though for the moment in a sketchy way) to our contention.

A major technological breakthrough (say nuclear electricity production) appears on the stage of production generally because of a supply push due to pressure groups formed by those who have developed the technology and by the business groups which want to profit from it (in certain instances also a specific demand pull may be present, e.g. the Kippur war and the subsequent oil shortage in the nuclear case). Were the new technology non-tragic we can assume that in the end its introduction would mainly depend on the advantages it shows *vis-à-vis* existing competing technologies. When the decision entails a tragic choice we have seen that the situation differs because of a sharp conflict of ethical values which make a public intervention necessary either to regulate the issue or to manage it directly. The lobby favouring a positive decision would of course try to avoid for as long as possible the opening of such a conflict or play down the importance of the risks to human life which the decision brings about.

Thus the lobby works in the direction of stability of the decision process because once the specific decision which is in its interest is taken, the pressure group would have no interest to change it and would go on trying to solve or to play down the conflict of values.

While the scientific and industrial pressure groups involved in the application of the risky technology would tend to aim, as it were, to stability through progress (or, more precisely, change), the voters would likely choose the status quo if asked to decide directly (say, through a referendum, like in Italy, on nuclear energy) on a critical question involving a deeply felt, though not necessarily a high, risk for life, such that it creates anxiety also because of the high cost of information. Different kind of lobbies, such as those of environmentalists and the like, would co-operate to avoid change. However, recourse to elections or referenda involves high costs (political, information etc.) so that the voters may have a powerful but often not a direct heard voice on specific issues.

The strategy of successive moves would however be fully exploited (though not necessarily consciously or through subterfuge) by politicians and bureaucrats. Adopting the simplest assumptions of the public choice model, each change would in fact provide the opportunity for increasing the bureaucrat's budget and the politician's votes.

To conclude, according to the Theory of Tragic Choices in order not to be too much hurt by the unavoidable conflict of values society adopts a cycle strategy, so as to change, as it were, the part of the social body which is hurt and give it some relief while another part is put under pressure for a certain period. By means of a very preliminary application of the Theory of Public Choice we have shown that, with the exception of voters, the other actors on the public stage would find it convenient for them to accelerate such a strategy of change beyond its soothing purpose, and increasing the social cost of the cycle strategy.

The next question is whether, and how, it is possible to avoid such an acceleration of the cycle strategy and to what extent may a given decision be turned from tragic to non-tragic. This is, however, a question we are going to deal with elsewhere.

EMILIO GIARDINA*

1. The Italian Tradition in Public Finance and the Theory of Public Choice

I believe we can agree with Professor Peacock as to the fact that, if his thesis regarding the importance of the historical perspective in the study of political economy were put to the vote by Italian scholars of public finance, it would receive a large majority, if not a unanimous consensus. In this regard it is symptomatic that only a few years ago these same Italian scholars celebrated the Italian public finance tradition in a specific conference on the subject, the proceedings of which are in course of publication.[1] But having taken due note of this position, we are compelled to ask a question: how is it that the seeds contained in this tradition have not given rise to a development in Italy of something analogous to the theory of public choice? Or: how is it that the studies following this approach – in particular, as far as what interests us here today, those on public sector growth – have taken root in Italy rather as a phenomenon of ideas imported from abroad than as the elaboration and extension of the thought of our own forebears?

Obviously this is not the place to attempt an exhaustive reply to this question, but we can attempt to identify some of the elements which may contribute towards the formulation of such a reply. This attempt must of course be taken at its face value, that is, as an attempt at a rough idea to be verified at some other time and place on the basis of more mature and more closely argued study.

First of all, we can put to ourselves the following question: with regard to the seminal distinction, into two opposite poles, elaborated by De Viti de Marco, between the absolute and the democratic state, interpreted, the first on the basis of a monopolistic model and the second of a co-operative model operating

* Professor of Public Finance, Università di Catania.
1. *Atti del Convegno sulla tradizione italiana di Scienza delle finanze*, Pavia, September 18-20 1984, forthcoming.

in accordance with the principles of competition,[1] just what importance did this have in leading Italian public finance studies along the lines that they took and in excluding certain alternative lines of research? The following hypothesis might hold good: this distinction into two opposite poles implies that the phenomenon of redistribution of wealth and that of the utilisation of public organisation for private purposes are typical of the absolute state. This probably led some scholars who were interested in going deeper into public decision processes in systems of representative democracy to neglect the above-mentioned phenomenon and to fail to take into consideration the possibility of elaborating models intermediate between De Viti's two poles – models with greater heuristic capacities than either of those two poles. If one wished to make a comparison with the development of studies of the different market types in price theory, one might say that the influence of De Viti's distinction had the effect of precluding the entry of the imperfect competition model into the analysis of the determinants of public sector activity. And one might ask whether this suggestion was not reinforced by the conviction, so authoritatively expressed in our own times by Milton Friedman, of the lack of importance of the realism of hypotheses and of the superiority of monopoly and pure competition as instruments for formulating appropriate predictions compared with the alternative models.[2]

We might also put to ourselves the question of the influence exerted on the lines of development of public finance studies in Italy, by Pareto's theory of power elites, by Gaetano Mosca's contemporary theory of a ruling class and by the distinction made by Pantaleoni between voluntary arrangements of a contractual nature and political arrangements of a coercive nature.[3]

1. ANTONIO DE VITI DE MARCO, *Il carattere teorico dell'economia finanziaria*, Rome: Pasqualucci, 1898; *Principi di economia finanziaria*, Turin: Einaudi, 1934 (English edition, *First Principles of Public Finance*, New York: Harcourt Brace, 1936).

2. We could perhaps read according to this key of interpretation the two final chapters in LUIGI EINAUDI, *Miti e paradossi della giustizia tributaria*, Third Edition, Turin: Einaudi, 1959 (First edition, 1938).

3. VILFREDO PARETO, *Les systèmes socialistes*, Paris: Giard, 1902; and *Trattato di sociologia generale*, Second edition, Florence: Barbera, 1923 (First edition, 1916); GAETANO MOSCA, *Sulla teorica dei governi e sul governo parlamentare*, Palermo, 1884;

The idea that, even in a representative democracy, power is exercised by a restricted ruling class leads certain scholars to fix their attention on conflictual relations between this class and the mass of the governed and to attempt to establish limits to the possibility of realising the aims (also of paternalistic control) of the former with respect to the resistance of the latter. The consequence of which is to distract attention from the study of the interactions and exchanges that can occur between the voter-taxpayer and the elected, between these and the broad category of public officials and finally between the latter and firms and households in their respective roles as suppliers of goods and services to the public sector and as users of the services and as receivers of welfare benefits.

Another element which could be taken into consideration – but I confess at once that I have greater difficulty in assessing its specific importance – is the rise to power of the fascist dictatorship during the third decade of this century. As a consequence, the study of collective decision-making in representative democracy became less immediately topical and some scholars were induced to investigate the problem of the model of a state which best reflected the principles, if not the practice, of the official fascist doctrine.

To return to Pareto, it seems to me that his influence on the Italian public finance tradition may also have operated in another direction, namely in that of placing excessively ambitious objectives before those studying the determinants of the public sector and thus leading to theories of little significance. His research into the laws of general sociological equilibrium led some of his followers to transfer the aim of identifying the general sociological laws for the functioning of political organisations to the field of public finance. The outcome was designs of exorbitant ambition, such as the research programme of Borgatta, at the beginning of his studies, for the scientific analysis of fiscal

MAFFEO PANTALEONI (with ANGELO BERTOLINI), 'Cenni sul concetto di massimi edonistici individuali e collettivi', in *Giornale degli economisti*, 1892, pp. 285-323, reprinted in *Erotemi di economia*, vol. II, Padua: Cedam, 1964, pp. 1-42, and the essays in vol. I; see also ROBERTO MICHELS, *La sociologia del partito politico nella democrazia moderna*, Turin, 1911.

phenomena, the low fruitfulness of which programme is demonstrated by the very fact that the author refrained from any attempt at a complete development of it.[1]

2. The Growth of the Public Sector

In the lectures that we have followed with such interest and with the usual enjoyment that comes from an acquaintance with his ideas, Peacock reconstructs many themes from his well articulated analysis of the public sector, made over many years, around the unifying theme of public sector growth analysed in accordance with the public choice approach, and he adds an extremely stimulating leavening of historical perspective. In making the ensuing comments, I shall follow the guidelines of his three-part division of the subject: first of all, the analysis of public sector growth; then the economic consequences of this growth; and finally the examination of the constraints which can be brought to it under a representative system of government. In my opinion, one of the first things to be observed with regard to Peacock's analysis of the growth in the dimensions of the state is the conclusion – in any case, as Peacock himself points out, widely recognised today – that the search for a general theory of this phenomenon is a chimera and that what scholars can do is work out the categories of the main influences on this growth and formulate so-called empirical laws, like those of Wagner or Baumol, to serve as departure points for the detailed analysis of particular aspects of the subject under study. This conclusion is all the more remarkable in that it has been stated by an author who, in his time, had elaborated a specific theory of his own, widely discussed in the relevant literature on this field and one which had the merit of causing the debate to be taken up once more in the postwar period.

But even under these constraints imposed on the research work, in Peacock's opinion the importance of one factor emerges, a full understanding of which is aided by the historical perspective,

1. GINO BORGATTA, 'Lo studio scientifico dei fenomeni finanziari', *Giornale degli economisti*, January and March 1920, pp. 1-24, 81-116.

148

in particular under the stimulus of the thinking of de Tocqueville. In Peacock's own words: "the growth [of the public sector] depends on the resolution of forces which are governed by human action and testable models must therefore embody a clear delineation of the participants in political decisions and what motivates them".[1]

The approach which derives from this allows Peacock, on the one hand, to make a critical assessment of the value of different explanations which have been given in the literature, by developing arguments which show the true range and limits of such explanations and, on the other hand, to overcome certain objections which the public choice approach may run into.

However, the central point of Peacock's contribution in the lecture dedicated to public sector growth seems to me to be his analysis of the thinking of de Tocqueville on the demand for redistribution of wealth. He develops this thought into a model which assumes that the growth in the ratio between the public sector and Gross Domestic Product is a positive function (a) of the extension of franchise and (b) of the inequality in the distribution of income; and he incorporates a mechanism based on the theory of the median voter which places a limit on this growth. Models of this kind are more general than those which take account only of the inequality of income distribution. It might seem that this more general character would have mainly a historical significance, since the vote has long been extended to all citizens in the western democracies. But this is not the case.

Peacock himself, in introducing the element of the expectations of the voter-taxpayer, indicates the present-day importance of electoral suffrage on the positive level of the explanation of the phenomenon of the growth of public expenditure, by pointing out the burden which, in a pay-as-you-go system of social security, the present generation of workers places on workers of the future generation who today lack the right to vote.

But the argument for the present importance of the model can be pushed still further. It is sufficient to note the increasing phenomenon of immigration of third-world workers, with the

1. See Lecture 2, p. 54.

accompanying claims for equality of rights and the acquisition of citizenship and the right to vote. One should also remember the proposal that has been debated for some considerable time in Italy, for the introduction of the postal vote for citizens resident abroad. All this amounts to a sort of *de facto* extension of suffrage to new categories of voters, belonging prevalently to the lowest-income classes.

The de Tocqueville-Peacock model may also have interesting extensions with reference to the mechanism incorporated into it which limits the growth of the state due to redistribution. This growth is supposed to cease when the point of universal suffrage is reached and the income of the median voter coincides with, or reaches a given ratio to, the average income. At this point it would seem that there is no longer room for policies of income redistribution as these would not earn the consensus of the median voter. But it is not necessarily so. One may in fact imagine redistributive actions at zero cost to taxpayers, by way of the sale of fractions of public property at particularly low prices to the beneficiaries, for example through the sale of shares in public corporations to be privatised, or the sale of public sector housing to the people who rent the houses. In these cases, the redistribution policies have the important feature that they earn the consensus of the electorate without giving rise to growth in the size of the state – indeed they cause a reduction in the public sector through the passage to the private sector both of (the income produced by) the assets sold and of the bureaucratic organisations which manage these assets.

It should also be observed that, in the case of situations in which the limits foreseen in the de Tocqueville-Peacock model have not been reached, it is not easy, at least on the present occasion, to specify the effects of redistributive measures, in so far as there could be opposition between political parties proposing to take such measures, and other parties making the traditional proposals for redistribution through taxes on the rich. In order to make a more precise statement, it would be necessary to define still further the voter's preference function, introducing in it arguments like, for example, the composition of the portfolio, and (why not?) the very size of the public sector.

Furthermore, if we also bear in mind, in accordance with the spirit of de Tocqueville's thinking, the importance of learning processes ("learning by doing"), we cannot neglect the fact that the distribution of shares of public property can cause changes in the attitudes of the voters themselves, who have their first experience of possessing certain kinds of property. One might say: *semel dominus, semper dominus*.

These considerations make it possible to point to a short-coming of the models of vertical redistribution, which I do not know whether Peacock's construction is capable of avoiding; it is the little weight that these models give to the direct action of politicians in influencing and moulding the voting attitudes of individuals. I am not referring to the phenomenon of fiscal illusion, so much as to activities aimed at modifying the very preference functions of voters. These models usually assume a one-way relationship from the electorate to those in power, and neglect the reverse connection which, as we have observed, can, under different circumstances, generate considerable effects. Furthermore, these models, just as, for that matter, the whole public choice approach – perhaps because it was developed with the experience of the United States particularly in mind – generally ignore the role which political parties can play in the collective decision-making process through the trust which they build up with the electorate, and the provision of compromise packages in the face of the variegated demands which the electorate makes. It is only recently that interesting perspectives have emerged in this direction.[1]

Returning to Peacock's model, having discussed its present-day importance in both its constituent elements, it is necessary to take into account other possible limitations. I do not propose to mention here the criticism according to which explanations like those of Peacock do not have a sufficiently general character with respect to the phenomenon of public sector growth, because we have already considered his thinking regarding the limited significance of every explanation of this phenomenon,

---

1. GIANLUIGI GALEOTTI and ALBERT BRETON, 'An Economic Theory of Political Parties', *Kyklos*, No. 1, 1986, pp. 47-65.

including his own. The criticism that concerns us here is above all the objection that, if public sector growth is considered to be endogenous with regard to the political process, it is hard to see how it can be expected that, in a situation of limited, not universal, suffrage, the median voter will agree to the extension of the vote to poorer persons. That is, he would be concurring in an institutional innovation which removes him from the decisive role he plays and which brings him a part of the burdens of the new redistribution caused by the broadening of the electorate.[1]

There is also the observation, according to which empirical evidence would show that a considerable part of public expenditure in western countries has been financed by taxes levied on the beneficiaries themselves.[2] The data for this evidence display extremely ambiguous traits – and Peacock for his part does not fail to warn against the procedures of empirical verification of models designed to explain public sector growth. But if these data were to be considered well founded and therefore valid for showing the falsity of the hypothesis that the demand for vertical redistribution represents an important factor for the explanation of the expansion of the public sector, there still remains a broad field for non-vertical (horizontal) redistribution to give substance to public choice studies which emphasise redistributive aims as being an important explanatory factor. We still rather regret that Peacock, who has carried out and supported some interesting analyses in this direction, did not find adequate precursors also in this regard, so as to offer us in these lectures yet another proof of his capacity for connecting the ideas of the past with our need to understand the present.

If I had been able to offer him a suggestion, I should have called his attention to the principle, laid down by Pareto, that "the intensity of a man's actions is not proportional to the gains and losses that these actions bring about". Since, as Pareto writes, "if you take one franc from each of one hundred men,

1. See for example Dennis C. Mueller, 'The Growth of Government: A Public Choice Perspective', *International Monetary Fund Staff Papers*, March 1987, pp. 115-49.
2. In addition to the bibliography referred to by Peacock, see also Diego Piacentino, *L'espansione delle finanze pubbliche nei paesi industriali*, Milan: Angeli, 1984.

these men will not react in defence of their own interests with as much vigour as one man would act, if he were stung into action by the desire to appropriate those hundred francs".[1] This principle is at the basis of present-day theories regarding pressure groups and log-rolling. It helps to explain why the electoral gains expected by politicians from competing groups of beneficiaries of public spending are greater than the loss of votes that they expect from taxpayers who have to bear the corresponding tax burdens.[2]

In this regard, it is worth noting that Pareto applied this principle, in a well-known passage in his *Course of Political Economy*, precisely to a proposal for electoral approval of a transfer of money to just a few people – a transfer which was to be charged to the broad mass of citizens.[3] In this passage the implication is clear of the existence of asymmetry in the reactions of individuals to proposals for the expansion of public expenditure with respect to proposals for the reduction of taxes. We can say then that Pareto was not only a precursor of pressure group theories, but that he also anticipated the reply to the objection that has been raised in contemporary literature to those theories, namely that they are not convincing because it is to be expected that the groups which press for increased expenditure will be offset by those who demand reductions in taxes.[4] In fact this

1. VILFREDO PARETO, *Cours d'économie politique*, Lausanne: Librairie de l'Université, 1896-1897, par. 1046. See also PARETO, 'The Parliamentary Regime in Italy', *Political Science Quarterly*, 1893, pp. 677-721, reprinted in PARETO, *The Ruling Class in Italy before 1900*, New York: 1950. The phenomenon had been pointed to by ANTONIO DE VITI DE MARCO, 'L'industria dei telefoni e l'esercizio di stato', *Giornale degli economisti*, September 1890, pp. 279-306 (quoted in MINISTERO DEL TESORO, *Relazione della Commissione per la verifica dell'efficienza e della produttività della spesa pubblica*, Rome: Istituto Poligrafico dello Stato, 1988, p. 23).

2. See most recently ASSAR LINDBECK, 'Redistribution Policy and the Expansion of the Public Sector', *Journal of Public Economics*, December 1985, pp. 309-28.

3. PARETO, *Cours*, op. cit., par. 1047.

4. See for all RICHARD A. MUSGRAVE, 'Leviathan Cometh – Or Does He?', in HELEN F. LADD and NICOLAUS TIDEMAN, eds., *Tax and Expenditure Limitations*, Washington, D.C.: The Urban Institute, 1981, pp. 77-120, reprinted in *Public Finance in a Democratic Society: Collected Papers of Richard A. Musgrave*, vol. II, Brighton, Sussex: Wheatsheaf, 1986, pp. 200-32; 'Excess Bias and the Nature of Budget Growth', *Journal of Public Economics*, December 1985, pp. 287-308.

GARY S. BECKER, 'Public Policies, Pressure Groups and Dead Weight Costs', *Journal of Public Economics*, December 1985, pp. 329-47, has pointed to two possible

objection does not take into account consolidated social attitudes
regarding tax equality, which make discriminations in taxation
treatment less acceptable to the electorate than those associated
with public expenditure. In order to understand the strength
of these attitudes it is sufficient to consider that in some countries,
for example Italy, they have been translated into principles
written into the constitution. Pareto himself invokes "the instinct
for equity and justice which exists in all human beings", which
could induce them to resist being despoiled, independently of
the loss that threatens them.[1]

3. The Economic Analysis of State Bureaucracy

From the lecture on the economic consequences of public sector
growth it seems to me that above all emphasis needs to be
placed on Peacock's judgement as to the limited nature of
certain present-day models of the bureaucracy which depend on
their restricted formulation of the arguments of the individual
utility function and his attempt to extend its range by utilising the
stimulus of the ideas of certain classical economists. In particular
he criticizes the excessive emphasis placed on the objective attributed to top bureaucrats, i.e. maximizing the budgets of
their organizations.

The dissatisfaction with the models aimed at explaining the
behaviour of the bureaucracy is very widespread, even if one
should not overlook the fact that the meagreness of the results
of the analyses and the narrow explanatory range are necessary
connotations of every attempt to open new paths of research.
This dissatisfaction seems also to derive from the impression one
has that certain limitations which characterize the models of the

factors of asymmetry between groups of taxpayers and beneficiaries of public expenditure: the diversity of political influence and the diversity of dead weight costs
in redistribution policies. But he makes no mention of a systematic asymmetry in
these factors with regard to the two groups.

1. Pareto in this regard stresses the need for politicians to base their action on a
moral idea. ASSAR LINDBECK, 'Redistribution Policy and the Expansion of the Public
Sector', *op. cit.*, points to the strong temptation of interest groups to dress up their
demand in altruistic and ideological terms.

bureaucracy in fact derive from the need to select those mo-
tivations of bureaucrats' behaviour which best lend themselves
to formalised treatment, rather than from their dispassionate
appraisal.

Peacock stresses the fact that the approach which interprets
bureaucratic behaviour with models analogous to those for
private entrepreneurs ignores the differences in the situations in
which the decision-maker is placed – differences which depend
on the diversity of the forms of organisation.[1] From his critical
evaluation of the contemporary literature, Peacock, as we have
seen, sees an urgent need to enquire along the lines followed by
certain precursors to produce a more articulated behaviour
model.

But generous and full of ideas as his attempt may be considered,
it must be said that it comes up against limitations which depend
on the restrictions of his assumptions about the institutions.
These limitations depend less on the arguments in the utility
functions of bureaucrats than on the constraints placed upon
the discretional behaviour of the latter.

In Professor Peacock's model, as we have learnt, the arguments of the utility functions of top bureaucrats are the number
of administrative staff, the amount of on-the-job leisure and the
fiscal residuum. The latter is definied as what is left over once
the members of the organisation have been paid their salaries,
the rates for which are fixed exogenously. This residuum can be
utilised to make the working environment more comfortable
and allow the official to run the organisation that much better.
One of the constraints on the maximisation of the utility function
is provided by the budget available, which consists of the sum
of the wages fund and the fiscal residuum. Thus a substitution
relationship is assumed to exist between these two possible
uses of the budget. Now, I am not sufficiently well informed

---

1. The remark is significantly analogous to that of MASSIMO SEVERO GIANNINI,
'Efficienza e produttività nella pubblica amministrazione', *Commenti della Rivista di
Amministrazione pubblica*, No. 3, 1988, p. 137, which underlines the need to differentiate between models of public structures, seeing that people continue 'to talk about
a public administration, that is about a creature that no one has ever seen and that
in reality is not a being but a plurality of beings'.

to make references to Great Britain, or to other foreign countries for that matter, but, as far as Italy is concerned, the institutional situation hypothesised, although perhaps appropriate for certain types of public organizations, is inappropriate to explain the behaviour of others (and I believe they are more numerous) in which the high official has no opportunity to use any bargaining-power or to decide any substitutions between the two items of expenditure considered.

The analysis of the consequences of the bureaucrats' behaviour is usually confined to the relationships between high officials and politicians. It is easy to understand why studies follow these lines, given that what is important for explaining the functioning of the political market here considered is the interaction between subjects endowed with decisional power – and, as far as the bureaucracy is concerned, these powers are concentrated in the hands of the high officials. But if this is true, even so it would be wrong to neglect the fact that all public servants, to however restricted a degree, have the power to exert influence in the public sector, by their bureaucratic behaviour in the political market. Individually considered, these powers are of minor or even minimum importance in comparison with those of high officials. But, taken as a whole, they can have total effects which are much more important than those of the high officials. It seems to me that Gordon Tullock was referring in some way to this problem when (after defining the system of top managers of corporations as a "black box", on account of our lack of knowledge of the interactions between their decisions and the constraints that they have to face), he observes that the "black box" of high officialdom is in effect composed of a nest of smaller black boxes contained within it.[1]

The effects on public sector growth of the behaviour of those bureaucrats who do not belong to the upper echelons can be studied under the category of X-inefficiency, seeing that these effects are imputable to the monopoly position that the state

1. GORDON TULLOCK, 'What Is to Be Done?', in THOMAS E. BORCHERDING, ed., *Budgets and Bureaucrats: The Sources of Government Growth*, Durham, N.C.: Duke University Press, 1977, pp. 275-88.

holds in the supply of public services. From this perspective the behaviour of these bureaucrats is comparable to that of workers in monopolistic enterprises. As top managers or proprietors who enjoy market power are able to cover company inefficiency through higher prices, they have less incentive to keep close control over the behaviour of workers; these finish up by enjoying wider discretionary powers, which in turn breeds inefficiency. But this analogy between public organisations and private monopolies is satisfactory only in part. In fact one crucial point is that public employees can bargain with the public "proprietor" or with a top manager in the bureaucracy (when this man becomes an accomplice of a politician) to get decisions liable to give origin to X-inefficiency. In other words, as the public choice school has not failed to underline, they operate in the electoral market and bargain over the benefits associated with their jobs with the support they can provide as voters.

Italian history in recent years is full of cases of this kind. One example will suffice: the composition, region by region, of the public sector bureaucracy does not reflect that of the total population of the country. There is a relatively heavier weighting of public servants originally from the south of the country. These – for reasons which would take too long to explain here, but which depend among other things on the difficulties of finding housing – have a strong preference for returning to their own region of origin. The pressures which arise from these preferences are transmitted effectively to the public policy-maker, with the consequence that there are staff surpluses in the south, and shortages in the public administration of the north, with consequent pressures to remove these shortages. The final result is an overall excess supply of staff in public organisations, in comparison with a situation in which the factors under consideration do not operate.

The functioning of this electoral market can be dealt with more fully if account is taken of the fact that political parties and trade unions can also be included among the contracting parties and that employment in the state organisation tends to be seen as a good in itself rather than as an input in the process of supply of public services: a fact which some economic models of the bureaucracy have in any case taken explicitly into consideration.

Given the fact that in these lectures we have been powerfully urged to consider the historical perspective, it is worth stressing the fact that various precursors dealt with this electoral market in their analyses of the problem of the municipalisation of public services. For Italy it suffices to quote the classic work of Giovanni Montemartini, but much of the scientific literature at the turn of the century that dealt with the problem of so-called municipal socialism in Britain, the USA, Germany and other countries contains interesting observations on the subject.[1]

A second point in Peacock's exposition that needs to be considered concerns the emphasis which he places on the fact that the bureaucracy plays a role not just in the electoral market, with reference to the bureaucrat-politician-voter nexus, but also in the market in which the bureaucrats enter into relationships with enterprises and families.

The importance of this point is such that all its potentialities should be considered. The set of illicit relationships which are found in the market in which bureaucracy and its suppliers meet cannot be left out of the picture. I do not know the extent of the phenomenon of public corruption in other countries. In Italy it is believed that it is very widespread and some scholars have dedicated time to an assessment of the turnover of corrupt politicians and public servants. As is well known, there are many attempts to work out an economic theory of corruption. These attempts have, among other things, highlighted the fact that there is not necessarily incompatibility between the objectives of the administration and those of the corrupters and that the "over-production" of services is not a necessary effect of illicit relationships. However, it seems to me of interest at this point to stress the way this phenomenon can play a part

1. GIOVANNI MONTEMARTINI, *Municipalizzazione dei pubblici servigi*, Milan: Società Editrice Libraria, 1902 (Second edition, 1917). Also GAETANO MOSCA called attention to the danger that local government bureaucracy may condition electoral competition and thus public choices made by the local governments: see 'La municipalizzazione dei servizi pubblici' (1902), reprinted in *Il tramonto dello stato liberale*, edited by A. LOMBARDO, Catania: 1971, pp. 239-45.

in public sector growth by way of at least two causal chains. First of all, if we assume a model for the formation of prices based on the criterion of full cost, the prices of goods acquired from the public sector will be increased by the amount necessary for the payment of the corrupt. In the second place, phenomena of X-inefficiency are caused, as there is an interest in choosing the productive combinations which maximise the expenditure, so as to increase the sum paid for corruption, which is normally proportional to expenditure. As can be seen, these are effects which may easily be fitted into the framework of well-known models of bureaucracy, but which have behavioural bases which render these models more realistic.

But we can also add a third path along which corruption can influence the amount of public expenditure. Peacock has referred to de Tocqueville's ideas on the way in which the rapid replacement of politicians in power, on account of the electoral competition, causes a growth in public expenditure; public intervention programmes targets are often badly carried out or left incomplete. Taking up this argument again, we can observe that the rapid succession of corrupt rulers has the effect that these people deliberate new, unnecessary, or even useless, expenses, aimed at replacing equipment or operations that are still in working order or to acquire further equipment that will not be utilised. This is because in order for the corrupt to "cash in", there must necessarily be expenditure, independently of the utility of the expense.

At the same time, corruption also works on the revenue side and, if the reduction of revenue can result in the reduction of public expenditure, illicit behaviour has effects in the same direction, thus reducing the effects on public sector growth.

To conclude, it seems to me that we can observe that the analysis that Peacock makes of the bureaucracy, and the role he assigns to it as an explanatory factor for the increase in the public sector, present greater congruity with the theory of interest groups than with the theory of demand for vertical redistribution of income from the richest to the poorest, which, as we have already observed, assumes a passive position on the part of politicians and bureacrats with respect to redistribution policies.

4. *Control of Public Sector Growth*

If we wish to find a mythological archetype to denote the inanity of the efforts made to control public sector growth, while stressing its huge size, no myth would be more appropriate than that of Sisyphus.

In the last lecture, Peacock's aim is to ascertain whether the historical perspective can help us to establish whether the labours of Sisyphus, to keep within the same metaphor, are likely to be successful or whether we are not rather condemned to see the boulder of growth in the size of the state constantly rolling back on us, following the effects of political and institutional reaction which our vain efforts generate.

To verify this, Peacock has selected two ways of limiting the growth in the public sector among the many put forward in the literature, that is to say, the balanced budget rule imposed by a revision of the constitution and the constitutional reform of the criterion of majority vote for the approval of the budget.

In the examination of the first proposal, for a constitutional revision of the constitution, a wide-ranging analysis is made of the reasons which justify the balanced-budget rule. These reasons can be summed up in the expression coined by Buchanan and Wagner: "democracy in deficit".[1] At the basis of these reasons is the thesis, which Ricardo himself had put forward, that the taxpayer is insufficiently aware of the equivalence between public debt and taxation, given that he does not discount, or discounts insufficiently, the burden of debt financing (interest and capital repayment).

So much has been written on this subject that it is difficult to open new perspectives. But if it is true, as has recently been affirmed, that economics is also a branch of rhetoric, old arguments can assume more convincing aspects if they are reformulated in a more solid theoretical framework.

---

1. James M. Buchanan and Richard E. Wagner, *Democracy in Deficit: The Political Legacy of Lord Keynes*, London: Academic Press, 1977. See also James M. Buchanan, Charles K. Rowley and Robert D. Tollison, eds., *Deficits*, Oxford: Blackwell, 1987.

Peacock points out the important distinction between the concept of fiscal illusion, which he defines as an error in the estimation which the taxpayer makes of the expected value of the total burden for debt financing, and the perception that he has of his contribution to this total burden – a perception which is the result of an assessment in conditions of uncertainty. And he observes that the authorities could use their power of control over the complexities of the structure and repayment dates of the debt, to produce the illusion that the debt is not less but more burdensome than the taxation.

The introduction of conditions of uncertainty into the analysis of the debt/tax alternative, adds an element which considerably increases the complexity of the explanatory models. The uncertainty may concern the future changes of a multiplicity of important economic variables in the problem under examination, the main ones being national income, population, tax law, the interest rate, the taxpayer's income and the length of his life. If I may be allowed to quote myself, in a Markowitz-type model, based on the hypothesis of maximisation of expected utility, I have shown that it is not possible to formulate unequivocal statements as to the taxpayer's preferences for one of two fiscal alternatives in conditions of uncertainty regarding the variables mentioned above. The ambiguity of the results remains even if the elements of distortion (such as the debt illusion) are introduced into the individual valuations, or else if account is taken of the aversion and propensity to risk.[1]

Peacock makes the important hypothesis that the debt illusion may diminish with the growth in the total tax burden, which we must suppose to be in some way correlated to public expenditure. This is because the readiness of the taxpayer to meet the costs of obtaining more information about the effects of the taxation system on his economic position grows *pari passu* with expenditure. In my model one of the assumptions made is that in order better to define the taxpayer's evaluations with respect to the two fiscal alternatives in conditions of uncertainty

---

1. EMILIO GIARDINA, 'Le preferenze del contribuente per il debito pubblico e per l'imposta straordinaria in condizioni di incertezza', *Annali della Facoltà di Economia e commercio dell'Università di Catania*, 1965, pp. 3-87

and to reduce the ambiguity of the results of the analysis the relationship should be considered between individual income and the public expenditure to be financed.

Empirical tests, as Peacock himself states, have not made it possible to resolve the question of Ricardian equivalence. But we must take note of the widespread awareness in public opinion in various countries regarding the growing burden of public debt, and we can take this fact as evidence, indirect though it is, of the hypotheses mentioned concerning the importance of the amount of public expenditure in producing the phenomenon of debt illusion.

Unfortunately the weight of the theoretical arguments and of the empirical tests regarding the thesis that the recourse to public debt provokes excessive growth in the public sector is fundamental for getting to grips with the problem of the advisability of, or the necessity for, a revision of the constitution which will impose the balanced budget rule as an instrument for the containment of public sector growth. In fact, in my opinion, it is not sufficient to demonstrate, as some scholars have done, the limited effectiveness of the instrument proposed to achieve the desired aim. Like every other economic problem, also in the case we are examining here, it is a question of the appropriate alternatives. The imposition of the balanced budget rule is acceptable, with all its defects and inefficiencies, if we believe that the advantages which it brings are greater than the costs associated with the size of the state and that the alternative means of containing this expansion are less effective, or that in any case a mix of control instruments, including the balanced budget rule, is the best solution to obtain the desired aim. As I said, unfortunately in order to make this assessment one cannot avoid making the difficult demonstration that the public debt, with the fiscal illusion it produces, is one of the principal causes of excessive growth in the public sector.

But before leaving this point, I believe that it is worth stressing the fact that it is possible to talk about public debt illusion in another sense, quite opposed to the one which Buchanan makes the basis of his idea of democracy in deficit. That is, in the sense indicated by Pareto, who maintains that public borrowing "is a way of despoiling those who delude themselves that they are being paid". In Pareto's opinion, in the long run, it is not the taxpayers who are subject to fiscal illusion, because they would not discount the tax burdens for servicing the public debt, but the creditors of the state who finish up by being despoiled by the state itself, especially as a result of that occult tax whose name is inflation, but also through conversions and various other manipulations which national debt bonds lend themselves to.[1]

Now it is clear that if this type of illusion is indeed at play, Ricardian equivalence – of the two financial instruments – disappears and the debt is revealed in truth as a means for broadening the politicians' discretion in decisions regarding expenditure.

The second remedy for the control of the size of the state, namely reform of the simple majority criterion for the approval of the budget, is analysed by Peacock in the light of Wicksell's thought. As Peacock notes, the Swedish economist was looking for a solution to the problem posed by de Tocqueville, regarding the extension of electoral suffrage, and the solution he offered was that of the near unanimity voting criterion. This criterion is nowadays invoked with the aim of preventing the excessive expansion of public spending resulting from the principle of simple majority, which makes it possible for a majority coalition to reduce the tax cost of public undertakings, by unloading a part of the cost of the expenditure onto a minority. Peacock makes two objections to this proposal for constitutional reform. The first is the paradox of the "hall of mirrors": with which procedure will the reform be approved? What voting criterion is acceptable to decide which voting criterion should be adopted? Is it realistic to suppose that the amendment of the constitution will be approved by a decision-making body which is self-limited by means of the criterion of simple majority?[2]

1. Vilfredo Pareto, 'Sugli effetti dei prestiti e delle imposte – (Lettere al Prof. Griziotti)' (1917), reprinted in Benvenuto Griziotti, Studi di scienza delle finanze e diritto finanziario, Milan: Giuffrè, 1956, vol. II, pp. 263-7. See also Pareto, 'Imposte, debito, carta moneta', L'Economista, March 28, 1920, reprinted in Battaglie liberistiche, Salerno: Società Editrice Salernitana, n.d., pp. 515-19.

2. The paradox of 'the hall of mirrors' recalls that considered by the constitutionalists regarding the possibility that a constitution may give rise to conditions requiring its own modification. Alf Ross, On Law and Justice, London: 1958, par. 16,

In the second place, Peacock notes, the plausibility of the rule of an almost unanimous vote depends on the nature and the weight of the explanations that are given for the expansion of the public sector. Anyone who points a finger at the factors which operate on the supply side will hold that the remedy under examination is ineffective and will propose others.

It seems to me that there will be no one who will not agree with this second point. But, if we develop the implications, we can show that it can be valid for defining the limits to the paradox of the "hall of mirrors". If we adopt an historical perspective different from that of Wicksell and we follow Pareto's reasoning which, as we have said, can be put at the basis of the contemporary theories on pressure groups and log-rolling, we find explanations of public sector growth within which it is plausible to suppose that even if a simple majority system of voting is in force, individuals will make an agreement to adopt more stringent voting rules. In fact, according to the theories referred to, the play of interests of individuals and groups gives rise to a situation which we can consider, in Buchanan's words, as a variation of the prisoners' dilemma with n-persons.[1]

Steve, who does not belong to the public choice school, has effectively described this situation with reference to the Italian context: ". . . within the sphere of parliamentary work there has been an increase in the weight of sectoral pressures, and thus a strengthening of the mechanism for the search for deals among the various groups which operate in parliament. It has thus become a common method to obtain a majority for an expenditure which interests a particular group, to offer in exchange a vote for an expenditure which interests another group. This game of *do ut des* is undoubtedly a basic reason for the uncontrolled expansion of public expenditure and for inflation. This is above all because by this method a situation is determined

makes appeal to the authority of the logician J. JORGENSEN, 'Some Reflections on Reflexivity', *Mind*, July 1953, pp. 289-300, to exclude any such possibility, and to maintain that the phenomenon of constitutional change is merely a socio-psychological fact, outside any juridical procedure.

1. James M. Buchanan, 'I limiti alla fiscalità', in *La costituzione fiscale e monetaria: Vincoli alla finanza inflazionistica*, Rome: Crea, 1983, pp. 17-34.

in which it is easy to obtain a parliamentary majority for decisions as to individual expenditures, but parliament as a whole and, more generally, society as a whole, absolutely does not agree with the overall volume of public expenditure. Each person has fought in order to have a particular expenditure which is of interest to him, but he finds the overall expenditure alien to his own judgement and his own interests and so tries to avoid a non-inflationary cover."[1]

It is thus reasonable to suppose that individuals can reach an agreement to renounce a system of voting which is damaging to all, or to accept a rule that goes beyond a simple majority, and can decide to exercise self-discipline. Various authors, starting from Elster, have, in cases like this, invoked the myth of Ulysses and the Sirens.[2] Human beings often seek to protect themselves from seductions which they know they otherwise cannot resist. The constitutional rules are precisely a method by which one binds oneself to political choices which one foresees one might later come to regret having made.

This argument may have some bearing even within the sphere of those explanations that derive from the thinking of Wicksell and de Tocqueville, which stress the demand for vertical redistribution. One limit to this kind of redistribution is provided by the restrictive effects that is has on the formation of the national income and, hence, on the income of the median voter. It is reasonable to suppose that the individual has expectations with regard to these effects, just as he has expectations with regard to his future income. It is clear that these expectations are surrounded with a halo of uncertainty. This means that no one knows with certainty who the median voter is. A whole collection of individuals may consider themselves to be in this position. If we find ourselves in a situation not far from the extreme case in which vertical redistribution policies come to an end, the voters who consider that they might be decisive and do not exclude a

1. SERGIO STEVE, 'Conclusioni', in EMILIO GERELLI and FRANCO REVIGLIO, eds., *Per una politica della spesa pubblica in Italia*, Milan: Angeli, 1978, pp. 223-31.

2. JON ELSTER, *Ulysses and the Sirens: Studies in Rationality and Irrationality*, Cambridge: Cambridge University Press and Paris: Editions de la Maison des Sciences de l'Homme, 1979.

possible reduction in their income, may, if they are averse to risk, decide to abstain from going along with the redistributive policies, by approving with the criterion of a simple majority the adoption of a constitutional amendment for a qualified majority.

5. Concluding Remarks

I should like to conclude these observations by noting that Peacock's lectures are pervaded by a juxtaposition of the force of interests on one side and the force of ideas on the other, in his explanation of social institutions. This runs like a sort of coloured thread through the different subjects that he deals with and binds them together. I have the impression that he has "overexposed" this juxtaposition, so as better to sell his product. Peacock is very critical of those economists, starting with Keynes, who are convinced that ideas prevail over interests and who are therefore inclined to offer their ideas to the Prince in order to change the world. But he does not hesitate to take a lunge or two at Hayek himself, who certainly did not share that proclivity. One might ask: is Peacock himself fully convinced of the force of his own idea that ideas have little force compared to the force of interests? And what are these lectures if not an essay in persuasion? But, perhaps, leaving aside the search for possible antinomies or paradoxes in Peacock's position, it might be useful for us to recall the thought of another precursor, as was exposed and commented upon by Luigi Einaudi. I am referring to Einaudi's essay devoted to original sin and the theory of an elite class in Le Play, in which he illustrates "the battle against the fundamental error of believing in the original perfection of mankind" conducted by the French scholar through all his work and the role of the elite class, that is "that which best interprets and actuates the constitution proper to men", the role which this class knows how to perform in order to lead society to prosperity.[1] Le Play's

---

1. LUIGI EINAUDI, 'Il peccato originale e la teoria della classe eletta in Federico Le Play' (1936), reprinted in *Saggi bibliografici e storici intorno alle dottrine economiche*, Rome: Edizioni di Storia e letteratura, 1953, pp. 309-43. RICHARD E. WAGNER, 'Chains or Opportunities? A Constitutional Odyssey', 1987 (mimeo), has recently made some

and Einaudi's position, it seems to me, can be summed up in a few words as follows: man is not born perfect and his instincts lead him to be selfish and even wicked. But the behaviour of the elite class, its moral example and the social institutions which this class is capable of devising may induce him to overcome his natural inclinations.[1]

With reference to our problem, we can conclude that interests condition the actions of men, but ideas also count. The space they may hold in determining social behaviour is by no means insignificant: indeed, as Einaudi reminds us, it is the space that lies between prosperity and the ruin of peoples.

important observations on the complete reversal of perspectives deriving from the abandonment of the concept of original sin (endorsed by the Founders of the Consitution of the United States of America) with regard to the general understanding of human nature and self-interest, and therefore of the properties of political power and of the limits of a constitution.

1. In a different context, from which the perspective of a governing class is absent, BUCHANAN and VANBERG have recently added some important elements which help to clarify the relationship between ideas and interests within the political process. They distinguish between the valuation and knowledge components of individual preferences (interests versus theories) and with reference to the latter they stress the importance that political debate can have in the process of collective choice, in particular in those of a constitutional nature: see VIKTOR J. VANBERG and JAMES M. BUCHANAN, 'Interests and Theories in Constitutional Choice', paper prepared for the Conference on 'Motivation for Constitutional Design and Reform', Niagara-on-the-Lake, Ont., November 6-7, 1987 (mimeo).

PETER M. JACKSON*

In his Mattioli Lectures Alan Peacock has in his customary style raised a set of interesting questions about the nature of the methodological foundations of our subject: this in addition to his main theme of placing public choice theory into historical perspective.

Historicism is a theme which pervades each lecture. From the question, is there a demand for historical perspective when studying public choice theory to the need for an historical and evolutionary approach to the examination of the growth and development of public sectors. In my comments I want to explore a little further some of these themes that Alan Peacock has presented to us. In particular I want to suggest that through its attempts to understand the nature of the world in which we live the public choice perspective provides economists with a richer, deeper and more relevant economics than does the dominant neo-classical paradigm. Indeed, as a result of studying economic processes, such as the growth of the public sector, public choice economists have made an attempt to provide the basis of a dynamic or evolutionary economics which emphasises "process" rather than the dynamic equilibrium of the long run which is the stock in trade of the neo-classical approach.

In the First Lecture the question was asked – is there a demand for historical perspective when it comes to our analysis of the theories of public choice? Can we study a subject in a meaningful way without reference to the work of the founding fathers? The answer must be yes because that is the way economics is taught in the majority of universities today. An emphasis on the techniques of economic and econometric analysis has, as Professor Peacock suggested, crowded out a treatment of the history of economic thought. The demand for "HET" is in many respects a derived demand. Students need to be demonstrated the usefulness of the history of thought. How will it contribute to an understanding of modern technique?

* Professor of Economics and Director of Public Sector Economics Research Centre, University of Leicester.

I am reminded of a statement that the late Harry Johnson made when discussing the importance of Keynes' *General Theory*. He referred to it as a "classic" within economic thought and then went on to define a classic as a book to which everyone refers and from which they frequently quote but a book which only a few have actually read![1] This to my mind was an unfortunate state of affairs in the early 1960s when Harry Johnson wrote his piece but I regret to say that things have become much worse. The average student today probably doesn't even know which set of books constitutes the classics. Students seldom refer to David Hume, Adam Smith, John Stuart Mill, Ricardo or Keynes. These are unknown names because they are relegated to the footnotes of textbooks and students do not read footnotes! Students today too often do not know the route to Schumpeter's lumber room.

But we cannot altogether blame our students. If blame is to be placed anywhere it must be with those of us who teach. My own view is that it is probably a mistake to have a compulsory course on the history of economic thought within the curriculum. Rather we could make our core courses in economic analysis much more interesting by referring to the historical antecedents of a particular theory or technique. In that way the history of thought serves to illuminate the present – it provides a perspective that is sadly lacking in modern economics: it gives our theories an origin, a grounding and a sense of evolution and development. It also provides our students with an invitation, if they should choose to accept it, to join a group of researchers who have a research agenda that is a logical progression of ideas. The role of the history of economic thought is not to study the mistaken theories of the past – rather it must be to:

(i) understand the nature of the "grand" problem that is to be solved;

(ii) incorporate methodological issues;

(iii) provide an appreciation of institutional factors.

---

1. HARRY G. JOHNSON, 'The *General Theory* After Twenty-five Years', *American Economic Review* (Papers and Proceedings), May 1961, pp. 1-17.

Today students have a bag of techniques, but what are the problems that these techniques might solve? What was the intellectual problem that troubled Smith – have we yet solved it? What were the problems that Keynes or Hume or Ricardo sought solutions for? Economics is more than solving constrained maximisation problems.

These are a means to an end. What we have tended to do is to forget what the ends are – to understand the ends of economic analysis we can profit from an understanding of the past and a search for origins.

In an influential and general study of the history of thought Michel Foucault makes the following observations:

> beneath the stubborn development of a science striving to exist and to reach completion at the very outset, beneath the persistence of a particular genre, form, discipline or theoretical activity one is now trying to detect the incidence of interruptions . . . the great problem presented by such historical analysis is not how continuities are established, how a single pattern is formed and preserved, how for so many different successive minds there is a single horizon . . . how the origin may extend its sway well beyond itself to that conclusion that is never given – the problem is no longer one of tradition, of tracing a line, but one of division, of limits; it is no longer one of lasting foundations, but one of transformations that serve as new foundations...[1]

In a Schumpeterian fashion the historical development of thought is through a process of creative destruction – the classics are either those epistemological acts of displacement and/or the works which fill the gaps left by the break with the past. Without an appreciative knowledge of the classics there is no unity of thought and there is only a narrow, partial, and blinkered research agenda. By establishing the wrong incentive structure within our discipline, by placing a higher value on technique rather than problem solving, we reduce the efficiency and effectiveness of our research agenda.

The subject matter of public choice reminds us of the fundamental problems which were of interest to the classical economists

---

1. MICHEL FOUCAULT, *L'archéologie du savoir* (1969), English edition, *The Archeology of Knowledge*, translated by A. Sheridan, London: Tavistock, 1972.

up to and including Keynes and his contemporaries. Equilibrium economics (both static and dynamic) and the technical apparatus that it subtends are but a narrow interpretation of the economic problem. Modern economic analysis is undoubtedly necessary to ensure and to demonstrate the internal logical consistency of our thinking but it too often represents a classic example of the public choice problem: of the means driving out or substituting for the ends of analysis. Technique has become an end whilst the original problem has too often been forgotten about.

Modern economics has lost the concept of "process" – the progression of an economy through real time rather than the fictitious time of dynamic equilibrium systems. A transportation through time requires the modelling of sequential decision making in which today's decisions are both history dependent and also formulated with reference to expectations of the future. This approach stands in sharp contrast to the simultaneous or once and for all time decision making which characterises the decision made within the neo-classical Walrasian system. In reality sequential progression of an economic system not only depends upon the objectives of decision makers but also upon a careful specification of the constraints (i.e. the institutions, rules, belief systems, etc.). It is those factors which will determine the "time pattern" of economic time series such as public expenditure. In the course of his lectures and in his previous work on public expenditures Alan Peacock has emphasised some of the factors which will influence such time patterns, e.g. interruptions to the pattern caused by upheavals and displacements brought about by paradigmatic shifts and major changes within the environment.

The public choice view of human action to which Alan Peacock refers in the Third Lecture and which was illustrated in that Lecture by reference to bureaucratic behaviour and in the Second Lecture by de Tocqueville's extension of the franchise, gives a much richer and more meaningful public sector economics. It provides us with a "fiscal sociology" – a term used recently by Musgrave[1] but having its origin in Schum-

---

1. RICHARD A. MUSGRAVE, 'Theories of Fiscal Crises: An Essay in Fiscal Sociology', in HENRY J. AARON and MICHAEL J. BOSKIN, eds., *The Economics of Taxation*, Wash-

peter,[1] Goldscheid[2] and Sultan.[3] Adoption of the term "sociology" is simply to remind us of the importance of human interdependencies and the complexities of human actions that take place within social and institutional structures to which human behaviour is not invariant. The thrust of much of the public choice theory is to draw attention to the complexity and intricacy of the mosaic of human action and it is a great pity that our colleagues who study private choice (with the odd exception such as Oliver Williamson)[4] have not chosen to recognise this.

For the most part private choice theory is not a theory of choice or of human action. It is instead a theory of markets and a very specific theory at that. Private choice theorists do not have an adequate theory of the firm nor do they actually have a theory of price determination. Instead, they have a series of heuristic fictions, shadowy figures and black boxes who behave in an "as if" world of metaphors not as individuals but as economic agents. The Walrasian model of prices which is the dominant paradigm ignores sequential decision making and is as authoritarian in its implementation through the auctioner as any Keynesian bureaucratic elite residing in Harvey Road.

In emphasising the public choice model of human action and through his examination of the historical antecedents of this line of enquiry Alan Peacock brings into centre stage the methodological issue of what is the best way for the economist to model human action. Answers to this question will determine the usefulness and effectiveness of economists in providing answers

ington, D.C.: Brookings Institution, 1980, pp. 361-90; reprinted in MUSGRAVE, *Public Finance in a Democratic Society*, vol. 2, Brighton: Wheatsheaf, 1986, pp. 175-99.

1. JOSEPH A. SCHUMPETER, *Die Krise der Steuerstaat* (1918), English translation, 'The Crisis of the Tax State', *International Economic Papers*, 1954.

2. RUDOLPH GOLDSCHEID, 'Staat, öffentlicher Haushalt und Gesellschaft: Wesen und Aufgabe der Finanzwissenschaft vom Standpunkte der Soziologie' (1926), partial English translation, 'A Sociological Approach to Problems of Public Finance', in RICHARD A. MUSGRAVE and ALAN T. PEACOCK, eds., *Classics in the Theory of Public Finance*, New York: Macmillan, 1958, pp. 202-13.

3. HERBERT SULTAN, 'Finanzwissenschaft und Soziologie', in WILHELM GERLOFF and FRITZ NEUMARK, eds., *Handbuch der Finanzwissenschaft*, Second edition, vol. 1, Tübingen: Mohr (Paul Siebeck), 1952, pp. 66-98.

4. OLIVER E. WILLIAMSON, *Markets and Hierarchies: Analysis and Antitrust Implications – A Study in the Economics of Internal Organization*, New York: Free Press, 1975.

to policy questions which must ultimately be at the heart of economic problems.

Surely Hume's "bundle man" is more interesting and more complex than passionless Pavlovian neo-classical economic man. Specification of the interests that motivate and propel individuals generates a richer set of testable hypotheses for the positive public choice theorist than does the neo-utilitarian approach. This can be illustrated from the theory of bureaucracy. In the Third Lecture the Niskanen model was presented and the Niskanen result that bureaucrats produce a level of output that is twice the social optimum was demonstrated. But that result is not a "fact". It remains a testable hypothesis that stands in contrast to an alternative hypothesis derived from a Humean system. Hume's bureaucrat, in sharp contrast to Niskanen's, might produce the socially optimal level of output if he/she values "duty", "trust" and "moral obligation" – these concepts enter the set of values to which Hume's passions refer.

A Humean public choice theory which I think Professor Peacock is inviting us to construct from the artifacts in the lumber-room is a research agenda as yet in its infancy. But it illustrates well the advantages to be obtained from a knowledge of the classics – the perspectives of Hume or Smith give a wide framework or broad canvas upon which the modern theorist can carry out more detailed work.

But a Humean public choice theory must also be balanced by the development of a Humean private choice theory. Let me try to illustrate this with reference to a point made in the Third Lecture. In that Lecture the Hayekian proposition that an enlarged public sector constrains human freedom and action was presented. But how does Hume's notion of freedom and liberty square up with Hayek's concept of negative freedom? I will speculate that it does not.

Hume saw the advantages of collective action and to the extent that unconditional moral obligation enters into the passions that motivate human actions then freedom can be extended through collective human action. It remains as an exercise for some scholar to find out if in Hume's scheme there is room for Isaiah Berlin's notion of positive freedom. If there is, then public choice *à la* Hume will provide a justification for a public sector different in shape and size to that which is based upon the neo-utilitarian approach.

The value placed upon collective action in the public domain is, therefore, not independent of the passions held in the private domain. This has to be remembered when we consider the question of the consequences of public sector growth. Much emphasis is placed by current public choice theory upon the deadweight losses and costs of the public sector on the private sector. However, empirical evidence tends to suggest that these deadweight costs are much smaller than is often supposed *a priori*. Moreover, if human passions place greater value upon the costs of co-ordination failures than deadweight losses, then, as Jim Tobin once informally pointed out, it takes a heap of Harberger triangles to fill an Okun gap.

What are we left with as a consequence of Alan Peacock's visit to the lumber-room? First, a reminder that de Tocqueville and Puviani provided additional hypotheses that might be integrated into current public choice theory. Second, and for me the most important, an invitation to reconstruct public and private choice theory through the incorporation of Hume's theory of human action. But I respectfully suggest that we need to go one stage further in the reconstruction: we must abandon the current public choice framework which adopts a Walrasian system of simultaneous decision making. Instead, we want a Wicksellian voluntary exchange model based on bargains and games and the constraints of rules. The name of Peacock is firmly associated with the notion of the "displacement effect" – I believe that through the Mattioli lectures Alan Peacock's name will become associated with another displacement effect this time within the history of thought – a displacement of neo-utilitarian public choice thinking by that based on Humean human action. These Raffaele Mattioli Lectures represent an epistemological threshold that suspends the continuous accumulation of knowledge in public choice theory and forces it to enter a new time.

FRANCO ROMANI*

I have known Sir Alan Peacock for the best part of a quarter of a century. In 1966 I had gone on a scholarship to Stockholm when I met Musgrave at a seminar. With great tact, he suggested that, seeing my interest was in public finance, perhaps I would have done better to go to Professor Peacock in York; no small compliment to Sir Alan for an illustrious American scholar to suggest, in the land of Wicksell and Lindahl, to an Italian student to go and further his studies in public finance within the York University whose guiding spirit (along with Jack Wiseman) was Sir Alan.

I remember that when I did first arrive, Sir Alan had me read one of his papers, as yet unpublished, regarding which I made some critical observations. As a result Sir Alan offered me a visiting lectureship and put me in charge of a seminar for public finance graduates.

Thus it was that I got the idea that Sir Alan appreciated the critical spirit. I shall therefore pass silently over the compliments for the excellent lectures that Sir Alan has given us and get straight down to critical brass tacks.

Professor Peacock's aim in these lectures has been to demonstrate that, for the student of public finance, "a knowledge of the history of economic ideas is desirable if not essential".[1] I do not think that the thesis has been satisfactorily proved. In reality, Sir Alan has proved a much more general thesis, namely that scholars should not limit themselves to the cultivation of their own academic back-garden, but should also devote themselves to good reading in general: a contention that would greatly have pleased Raffaele Mattioli. It would be extremely difficult, in a course of history of economic thought, to bump into a name like de Tocqueville. Only Schumpeter's voracious appetite for good reading explains why – for a few brief lines – the name of Alexis de Tocqueville appears in his *History of Economic Analysis*.[2]

* Professor of Economic Policy, Università di Roma «La Sapienza».

1. First Lecture, p. 27.

2. JOSEPH A. SCHUMPETER, *History of Economic Analysis*, edited by ELIZABETH BOODY SCHUMPETER, New York: Oxford University Press, 1954, pp. 432-3.

Sir Alan's frequent references to Hume and Smith – who certainly have a great role to play in an ideal course of economic thought – is also a reference to men of immensely wide interests, from philosophy to political theory, jurisprudence and science. Perhaps precisely because they had these groundings they could make their contributions to economic thought. And Professor Peacock was certainly right when, in his Inaugural Lecture at the University of Edinburgh in 1957, he said that we do not emulate Adam Smith's example simply by being authorities on what he wrote.[1] Perhaps we can emulate him if we try, insofar as the modern explosion of knowledge allows us, to broaden our field of interests as much as possible. This is particularly (though not exclusively) true for public finance, the problems of which lie at the centre of the theory of the state and therefore at the centre of moral and political philosophy. It is no chance that philosophers read economists while economists return the compliment much more rarely.

Shall we have to wait until another moral philosopher, after Adam Smith, comes along to re-establish our discipline? The theory of public goods, reformulated in terms of the prisoner's dilemma, is at the root of a large part of the political philosophy of our times. As is well known, the contractarian theories (from Hobbes on) represent the state as a solution to situations of the prisoner's dilemma type. Recently I had occasion to see studies, highly sophisticated from the point of view of economic analysis, written by philosophers (see, for example, Jean Hampton, who among other things is the author of a pioneering monograph on Hobbes) who put the question of whether public goods must necessarily be modelled in terms of the prisoner's dilemma. This is not simply an academic problem, because, as de Jasay wrote recently, and he is a non-academic who is well read in various fields:

If there is no inevitable public goods dilemma, and the contention that there is one – a basic proposition on which hinges the super-

1. See ALAN T. PEACOCK, 'From Political Economy to Economic Science', Inaugural Lecture as Professor of Economic Science, University of Edinburgh, *University of Edinburgh Gazette*, 1957.

structure of modern political thought – is a delusion, why is society organized as if private contracts were impotent to commit people to certain critical kinds of co-operation, and why does command play the role it does? ... if overcoming the conflict between private and public good is not the irreplaceable function one thought political institutions had to fufil, have they any other? Or are they just a bad habit, a slack letting go of individual responsibility one had learnt to indulge in but could unlearn?[1]

These are problems of great interest to which the economists with their mathematical armoury can make useful contributions. However, what worries me, from the strictly corporative view-point as an economist, is when the agenda for research is fixed by other disciplines. I get the impression that by now the much talked of "imperialism" of economic science is a legend. Or, if it is partly true, it is perhaps to be hoped that what will happen to us is what happened to the Roman occupants of ancient Greece: they became hellenised. Just how did this situation with economics come about? I am inclined to agree with Sir Alan when he detects as one of the causes of the misfortune (represented for him by the abandonment of the history of economic ideas and for me by something bigger) "the increase in the demand for economic advice as a contribution to the solution of policy problems".[2]

Paradoxically, one could also say that economic science has been spoilt by its successes, which have raised economists to the position of chief advisers to a prince, with the result that the agenda for research in economics is fixed by the practical day to day problems of politicians or, as Adam Smith said:

these insidious and crafty animals, vulgarly called statesmen or politicians, whose councils are directed by the momentary fluctuations of affairs.[3]

1. ANTHONY DE JASAY, *Social Contract, Free Ride: A Study of the Public Goods Problem*, Oxford: Clarendon Press, 1989, p. 125.

2. First Lecture, p. 7.

3. *An Enquiry into the Nature and Causes of the Wealth of Nations* (1776), Glasgow Edition of the Works and Correspondence of Adam Smith, vol. 2, edited by R. H. CAMPBELL, S. SKINNER and W. B. TODD ANDREW, Oxford: Clarendon Press, 1976, IV.ii.39.

Furthermore the economists' worldly success has come about along with princes of parliamentary democracy, that is, with particularly shortsighted princes insofar as the length of their perspective is at most that of a single legislature. Is it all that surprising if in this context we economists have lost sight of all historical perspective?

One piece of good fortune that has come the way of our discipline is that economists are going a bit out of fashion as councillors to the prince. I read in the *Wall Street Journal* the other day that on one occasion President Reagan – a man who surely knows all about fashion – asked: "Do we need a Council of Economic Advisers?" It may be that when economists feel themselves driven away from the high tables of the prince, they will get back on the road, if for no better reason than to snub the princes who ignore them, by showing these lordlings that they are simply coachmen-flies at the head of economic and social movements far profounder and longer-lasting than scientists are able to divine, but not princes.

In this light it is perhaps also possible to explain why the public choice school has been so successful. Most of the scholars in this school are declared enemies of the prince, to whom they often refer as Leviathan, and want at all costs to tame him and, in my opinion, it may be no mere coincidence that the very period in which this school has held sway is the one in which a so-called crisis in economic theory has occurred.

But I should like to move on to the discussion of some of the specific points dealt with by Professor Peacock.

I believe that the hypothesis, attributed to Stigler, according to which state intervention increases when the state has a comparative advantage over private enterprise in supplying certain services may go further than Sir Alan believes towards an explanation of social expenditure made by the private sector. The main reason is the increasing need for economic security which characterises modern industrial and post-industrial societies in all their complexity. Now, no one can provide economic security all on his own. It is possible for each individual to have security only if other individuals or groups of individuals agree, in certain circumstances, to share their incomes with him or her. Supplying security becomes almost necessarily a collective enterprise so that it is necessary to have recourse to coercion. But why has the demand for economic security increased? To answer this question I too would like to turn to de Tocqueville. (Without doubt Sir Alan will not disapprove of my choice of authority, since, apart from anything else, this only goes to strengthen his main thesis.) I wish to refer to the memoir on pauperism that de Tocqueville presented to the Cherbourg Academy in 1838, just after he had finished his work on democracy in America.

The problem which de Tocqueville puts forward is to try to explain how it was that, in his time, there seemed to be more poor people in rich societies than in poor ones. His comparison is between Portugal and Spain on the one hand and England and France on the other. He considers it useless to embark on a detailed comparison between these countries and proposes, to use Peacock's expression, "a grand design". He begins with the feudal period and observes that, in those times, the Third Estate did not yet exist and there were only two classes, those who worked the soil without owning it and those who owned it without working it.

As for the first group of the population, I imagine that in certain regards its fate was less deserving of pity than that of the common people of our era . . . Their means of subsistence was almost always assured; the interest of the master coincided with their own at this point.

The other class presented the opposite picture. Among these men hereditary leisure was combined with continuous and assured abundance. I am far from believing, however, that even within this privileged class the pursuit of pleasure was as preponderant as is generally supposed. Luxury without comfort can easily exist in a still half-barbarous nation. Comfort presupposes a numerous class all of whose members work together to render life milder and easier. But, in the period under discussion, the number of those not totally absorbed in self-preservation was extremely small. Their life was brilliant, ostentatious but not comfortable . . . If we look carefully at the feudal centuries, we will discover in fact that the great majority of the population lived almost without needs and the remainder felt only a small number of them. The land was enough for all needs. Subsistence was universal, comfort unheard of . . .

As time passes the population which cultivates the soil acquires new tastes. The satisfaction of the basic necessities is no longer sufficient. The peasant, without leaving his fields, wants to be better housed and clothed. He has seen life's comforts and he wants them. On the other hand, the class which lived off the land without cultivating the soil extends the range of its pleasures; these become less ostentatious, but more complex, more varied . . . A greater number of men who lived on the land and from the land leave their fields and find their livelihood by working to satisfy these newly discovered needs. Agriculture which was everyone's occupation is now only that of the majority. Alongside those who live in leisure from the productivity of the soil arises a numerous class who live by working at a trade but without cultivating the soil.

Each century extends the range of thought, increases the desires and the power of man. In order to satisfy these new needs, which cultivation of the soil cannot meet, a portion of the population leaves agricultural labour each year for industry.

If one carefully considers what has happened in Europe over several centuries, it is certain that proportionately as civilization progressed, a large population displacement occurred. Men left the plough for the shuttle and the hammer; they moved from the thatched cottage to the factory . . .

What has been, what is, the consequence of this gradual and irresistible movement that we have just described? An immense number of new commodities have been introduced into the world: the class which remained in agriculture found at its disposal a multitude of luxuries previously unknown. The life of the farmer became more pleasant and comfortable; the life of the great proprietor more varied and ornate; comfort was available to the majority. But these happy results have not been obtained without a necessary cost . . .

When almost the entire population lived off the soil great poverty and rude manners could exist, but man's most pressing needs were satisfied. It is only rarely that earth cannot provide enough to appease the pangs of hunger of anyone who will sweat for it. The population was therefore impoverished, but it lived. Today the majority is happier, but it would be on the verge of dying of hunger if public support were lacking.

Such a result is easy to understand. The farmer produces basic necessities. The market may be better or worse, but it is almost guaranteed: and if an accidental cause prevents the disposal of agricultural produce, this produce at least gives its harvester something to live on and permits him to wait for better times.

The worker, on the contrary, speculates on secondary needs which a thousand causes can restrict and important events completely eliminate . . .

The industrial class which gives so much impetus to the well-being of others is thus much more exposed to sudden and irremediable evils. In the total fabric of human societies, I consider the industrial class as having received from God the special and dangerous mission of securing the material well-being of all others by its risks and dangers. The natural and irresistible movement of civilization continuously tends to increase the comparative size of this class. Each year needs multiply and diversify, and with them grows the number of individuals who hope to achieve greater comfort by working to satisfy those new needs rather than by remaining occupied in agriculture. Contemporary statesmen would do well to consider this fact.

To this must be attributed what is happening within wealthy societies where comfort and indigence are more closely connected than elsewhere. The industrial class, which provides for the pleasures of the greatest number, is itself exposed to miseries that would be almost unknown if this class did not exist . . . The more prosperous a society is, the more diversified and durable become the enjoyments of the greatest number, the more they simulate true necessity through habit and imitation. Civilized man is therefore infinitely more exposed to the vicissitudes of destiny than savage man . . .

The progress of civilization not only exposes men to many new misfortunes; it even brings society to alleviate miseries which are not even thought about in less civilized societies . . .

If all these reflections are correct it is easy to see that the richer a nation is, the more the number of those who appeal to public charity must multiply, since two very powerful causes tend to that result. On the one hand, among these nations, the most insecure class continuously grows. On the other hand, needs infinitely expand and diversify, and the chance of being exposed to some of them becomes more frequent each day.

We should not delude ourselves. Let us look calmly and quietly on the future of modern societies. We must not be intoxicated by the spectacle of its greatness; let us not be discouraged by the sight of its miseries. As long as the present movement of civilization continues, the standard of living of the greatest number will rise; society will become more perfected, better informed; existence will be easier, milder, more embellished, and longer. But at the same time we must expect an increase of those who will need to resort to the support of all their fellow men to obtain a small part of these benefits. It will be possible to moderate this double movement; special national circumstances will precipitate or suspend its course: but no one can stop it. We must discover the means of attenuating those inevitable evils which are already apparent.[1]

The conclusion I personally wish to draw from de Tocqueville's teachings is that problems of economic security of this size could hardly be dealt with by the market – i.e. mainly by contracts of private insurance.

Without going into a discussion about the numerous failures of the market which characterise insurance, it may suffice to ask ourselves which insurance companies could stand up to a major depression. I have not the time available today, or to be more frank, I am not able to illustrate the way in which this demand for security has been translated into supply, so I will limit myself here to the observation that it was also in the interest of the privileged members of so-called capitalist societies to set up this great network of security which has made an economic system based on private property and market mechanisms acceptable to the majority of the population. This demand for economic security still permeates modern societies to the deepest levels. To give an example not linked up with the contingent requests of various political movements I should like to call your attention to the philosophical thought of our times. Think, for example, of Rawls, one of the most influential philosophers of the present day. What is his theory of justice if not a proposal for a gigantic social insurance operation? Certainly, I have not proved my thesis. However, I think I can claim that, with regard to economic security, Stigler's hypothesis of the state's comparative advantage, at least as far as the past is concerned, should not be dismissed too lightly. Of course, it may be that in future comparative advantage switches back in favour of the private sector, but this could only reconfirm Stigler's hypothesis.

---

1. Quotation from *Tocqueville and Beaumont on Social Reform*, translated by C. DRESCHER, New York: Harper and Row, 1968.

I should now like to go on to the discussion of other points from the lectures. I should particularly like to consider the electoral redistribution model. Sir Alan's analysis is brilliant, full of suggestions and ideas which will provide us all with interesting and enticing food for reflection. However, in my opinion, one problem seems to me not to have been fully faced up to. It is this: universal suffrage (at least for males) has been a reality in the western world for a long time back. As the heavy growth of the public sector has come about mainly since the Second World War, how is it possible to give such a great amount of interpretative importance to the electoral redistribution model? I should like to put forward a few conjectures in this regard.

The first is the following: as long as capitalist society remained simply divided structurally between the capitalists and the working class, the struggle for redistribution occurred above all in the sphere of the labour market. As is well known, the workers managed to organise themselves and to turn the trade union into a powerful monopolistic instrument, capable of exercising a very strong influence on the fixing of wages. Naturally, recourse was also made to the state. Social legislation was introduced (compulsory accident and unemployment insurance, workers' pensions, hospital care etc.). Progressive taxation was instituted (incidentally I should like to suggest to Sir Alan that he read again the chapter in De Viti de Marco's *Principles* regarding the political theory of progressive taxation).[1] However, the increased role of the state was held in check by the principle of the balanced budget. Heavy redistribution policies were soon to come up against the resistance of those hit by taxes and, in any case, the opportunity to introduce taxation systems was limited by the negative effect these had on incentives. (But Professor Peacock has spoken admirably about the limits of fiscal instruments for the purpose of redistribution.) What I am trying to maintain is that, with a uniform working class, the line of least resistance was that of obtaining advantages from

1. ANTONIO DE VITI DE MARCO, *Principi di economia finanziaria*, Turin: Einaudi, 1934; English Edition, *First Principles of Public Finance*, translated by E. P. MARGET, New York: Harcourt, Brace, 1936, Chapter 12.

redistribution in the labour market, rather than through state-controlled redistribution. In any case, as far as the most radical wing of the working class was concerned, the state was there to be overthrown (revolution) rather than put to use. However, as we all know, one of the most important aspects of the so-called post-industrial society is the disappearance of the classes. Workers and capitalists cease to be homogeneous classes and break up into sub-classes, into small groups with diverse interests. This fragmentation implies the abandonment of all ideas of the class struggle, whether on the part of the workers or the capitalists, and the acceptance of a reformist line of approach. That is to say, a great many pressure and interest groups get formed which, among other things, as Olson would say, being small, are easier to organise and which turn to the state for favours and privileges. All this happened in a context in which the role of the state alone had become of great importance for the good functioning of the economic system (the state had become the guarantor of full employment), furthermore it was free of all budget constraints according to Keynes' precepts.

I have to confess that I do not know how to test out these conjectures of mine: perhaps they cannot be subjected to refutation and are therefore simply meaningless propositions. However, the problem remains of explaining, a little better than the electoral model is able to do, just why there has been such a strong expansion of the public sector since Second World War. If my conjectures make some sense, they may serve as a further test of Stigler's hypothesis of the state's comparative advantage. Up to a certain point it was easier to obtain advantages in terms of redistribution by acting on the labour market, so the struggle focused principally there. When the comparative advantage of acting in this way ceases, then one turns to the state. I have put forward some conjectures as to why this should come about. But I could also produce more orthodox ones which furthermore would not be incompatible. For example, it might be said that, if prices and wages are given the strategic function of modifying the distribution of income, then they are no longer used to balance supply and demand. But if there is no equilibrium between supply and demand in the market, then tensions develop:

adjustments will come about mainly through variations in production and employment and thus situations of underproduction and underemployment may be brought about. One of the interpretations offered by economists to explain why these imbalances can become firmly established is the following.

Let us suppose that an economy is in a state of disequilibrium and that on this account there are workers without employment. The fact that these people are out of work involves a reduction in their purchasing power. This causes a drop in demand which leads producers to turn out less than they could if they were not limited by reduced demand. However, if the workers were not unemployed they would consume more and they would thus make it possible for producers to produce more and thus to employ more workers. But, as producers base their plans on the effective demand of employed workers and not on the potential demand, which includes the demand which there would be if the unemployed found work, the situation is stalled at a low level of production and employment. This trap is very similar to the prisoner's dilemma.

In this context Keynes proposed the solution should be to increase demand artificially by means of a budget's deficit, so that the discrepancy between effective and potential demand, due to the erroneous information provided by a broken-down price-system, would be filled. The solution was sensible and the "patch" very soon gave proof of its effectiveness. Hence the success of Keynesian economics. However, the acceptance of the Keynesian strategy had macroscopic political consequences.

In the first place the role of the state became enormously important for the good working of the economic system (the state became the guarantor of full employment).

In substance the system brought into being was as follows: when the state takes on responsibility for full employment, the workers, on making their bids for pay-increases, do not have the least need to worry about the possible consequences these bids may have on employment. Therefore they try to obtain improvements in their living standards which are in excess of their real increases in income. On the other hand, employers have no great interest in resisting the workers' bids, because, even if they realise that by accepting them, the costs of production will inevitably rise, they feel confident that the state, by way of appropriate financial policies, can guarantee a demand such as to allow them to sell their product at higher prices (and thus allow them to meet the higher costs). In this way wages and prices start chasing each other. In fact, when the workers begin to notice that their wage increases are been cancelled out by the increases in prices, they are induced to claim further and still bigger wage increases.

However, a process of this kind does little to modify the distribution between profits and wages. A redistribution of wealth through prices and wages ends up by losing all its bite. To obtain redistribution advantages, it is inevitable that this be done through government policy, chiefly by means of a policy based on taxes and expenditures. So we are back at Stigler's hypothesis of comparative advantage.

But I see that I have gone beyond my time. All that remains for me to do is to thank Professor Peacock for giving us this wonderful analysis concerning the problems of public choice, which has been so packed with suggestions and observations by which we have been intellectually enriched.

VITO TANZI*

For many economists public choice analysis is a major new development in economics, a development that, recently, has acquired enough status and respectability to justify the giving of the Nobel Prize in Economics to one of its major exponents. The new Nobel laureate, Professor James Buchanan, has himself always recognised his debt, in shaping his ideas, to the Italian school. However, many of those who consider themselves public choice analysts are unlikely to be fully aware of that school or to be fully appreciative of the impact that it has had on public choice especially through Professor Buchanan's writings. It is for this reason that Professor Peacock's Mattioli lectures are welcome.

In his scholarly way, and with the benefit of the kind of insight that comes from having been a major contributor to public finance over several decades, Peacock illustrates, in these lectures, the need to place public choice analysis in a historical perspective. By implication he also illustrates the potentially large cost of intellectual provincialism in time and in space. He focuses mostly on "provincialism in time", that is on the blinkers that we put on our intellectual vision when we assume that there is little that we can learn from any writing older than a few years. This kind of provincialism is widespread in today's economic profession although it is interesting to read through these lectures that Marshall and Pigou were not immune to it, and especially Marshall may have given respectability to it.

In these beautifully written lectures, Peacock shows just how much the field of public choice owes to the writing of some of the masters of the past. Perhaps less forcefully than I would have liked, he also makes the point that we could have benefited much more from their insights and perspectives had we paid more attention to their writings. He rightly regrets that few economists have ever read de Tocqueville's relevant writing on public choice. Peacock's lectures are more concerned in showing the historical heritage of public choice analysis than in showing

* Director, Fiscal Affairs Department, International Monetary Fund, Washington, D.C. and President of the International Institute of Public Finance.

how much of that heritage might have gone lost because of provincialism. Just how much more gold could have been mined by a greater attention to past writing? This is a question worth asking. Unfortunately, we may never fully know the answer.

The Italian contributions that he mentions were made for the most part more than 70 years ago. They were also made in Italian, a language that most Anglo-Saxon economists, who have dominated the economic field in this century, could not read. As a consequence, much of what was discussed in the Italian literature, for example, the discussions of the so-called Ricardian equivalence or the various views of the state, was totally ignored by recent writing. Thus, recent economics has rediscovered in several instances what had already been known to the Italian school.

As a graduate student in economics at Harvard in the early 1960s, I witnessed the lack of interest towards the history of economic thought in that great university that was surely at the forefront of economic research. There was also little or no interest in learning foreign languages. The assumption was that all that was important in economics was being said at that time and, of course, it was being said in English. This was true in a university where Schumpeter, who had been one of its influential members, had called attention to the benefits of occasionally visiting the "lumber room" of old ideas, as Peacock reports. What is often not recognised by the profession is that much of the writing that is done in any one period and in any one place is very much influenced, whether the writers are aware of it or not, by the institutions and the political winds of that period. In other words, we tend to direct our research towards what is fashionable at that time. And what is fashionable is influenced by the politics and the institutions of that time. These factors influence even the kind of research that we may consider as "theoretical" or "pure". The visit to the "lumber room" gives us a glimpse of intellectual experiments conducted under different institutions and/or political winds. Many of these experiments are likely to be irrelevant but some may be illuminating.

Thanks to a sabbatical year and a research grant from the

Bank of Italy, 17 years ago I had the opportunity of spending a few months in Italy reading the contributions of some of those who made the Italian *Scienza delle Finanze* an important school. These were enjoyable months although, in terms of specific output, they were not very productive months.[1] When I returned to Washington, I was drawn into a new and more demanding job. As a university professor I could have justified spending time writing on the Italian school. As an executive in a leading and very busy international institution I could not. However, what I learned from reading the Italian classics greatly influenced my thinking and my later writing, especially in relation to developing countries and in relation to the usefulness of the normative approach to public sector behaviour which has influenced public finance texbooks. I felt that the Italian school was often much more relevant to understanding the problems of the role of the public sector in Latin America than some of the theories that I had learned at Harvard. Somehow, Samuelson's "pure theory of public expenditure" seemed to have less to contribute to my understanding of the public sector behaviour in Latin American countries than Puviani's or Fasiani's work. This, I believe, is what Peacock is saying through his lectures.

In citing Schumpeter on the need to occasionally visit the "lumber room" of old ideas, Peacock also mentions Schumpeter's warning about not staying too long in that room. This is also good advice. The usefulness of old ideas is not often seen by taking a course or reading an occasional book on the history of economic thought, or by specialising on it, but by the occasional reading of the relevant classics themselves. When this is done by economists who are actively involved in current problems or in current research, the potential benefits of these occasional visits may be substantial. Old ideas can be illuminating but they can also be stifling. Long visits to the "lumber room", especially by those who are not involved with current problems

1. An article that I wrote at the time, based on the reading that I had done, has remained unpublished. See *Toward a Positive Theory of Public Sector Behavior: An Interpretation of Some Italian Contributions,* Fiscal Affairs Department Working Paper, Washington, D.C.: International Monetary Fund, November 1980 (mimeo).

or current research, may lead to the alternative and equally wrong view that there is nothing new under the sun. When this happens there may be a tendency to continue repeating those ideas even when they have become obsolete. In that case, as Keynes pointed out, we may become slaves of dead economists.

BIOGRAPHY OF ALAN PEACOCK

1. Biographical Note

ALAN TURNER PEACOCK* was born on 26th June 1922 at Ryton-on-Tyne, then a village on the outskirts of Newcastle-upon-Tyne, the son of Alexander Peacock, Lecturer in Zoology at Armstrong College (University of Durham), Newcastle and Clara. His father was appointed to the Chair of Zoology at University College, Dundee (then part of the University of Saint Andrews) in 1926. Peacock received his school education at the Grove Academy, Broughty Ferry (a suburb of Dundee) and Dundee High School, thus becoming a Scot by absorption. On the outbreak of the 1939-1945 War his father advised him to enter university a year earlier than usual and he enrolled at University College, Dundee and later at the United College in Saint Andrews itself. He began to specialise in Political Economy and History but his studies were interrupted by war service in the Royal Navy when he was called up in 1942.

His period in the Royal Navy was not without incident. As an Ordinary Seaman he served on East Coast convoys, and shortly after he became an officer in the Naval Intelligence Service in 1945 into which he had been recruited because of a knowledge of German. He was torpedoed in a naval action off Les Sept Iles on the coast of France, but was lucky enough to be picked up by a British destroyer returning to Plymouth. The rest of his time at sea was on convoys to North Russia but for two operations to as far north as Spitzbergen. After VE day, he was sent to the naval occupation forces in Kiel before returning to university late in 1945, by that time married to Margaret Astell-Burt, also a student at Saint Andrews and with one child. He was awarded the Distinguished Service Cross for his intelligence work in the Arctic Ocean.

The Royal Navy ran a series of correspondence courses through The College of the Sea, London, which was originally set up as an extra-mural college for merchant seamen. In 1944, Peacock enrolled for a revision course in Economics while still

* This biographical note is based on information kindly provided by Professor Alan Peacock.

at sea, and found himself writing essays for one of their war-time tutors who happened to be Arthur Cecil Pigou who had just retired from the Chair of Political Economy at Cambridge. This was a strange experience. The essays were written aboard ship in heavy seas without access to a library, and travelled over six hundred miles from Scapa Flow to Cambridge where they were corrected and commented on by the famous man. The comments seemed to assume that the student was more comfortably situated near the equivalent of the Marshall Library! Peacock benefited very greatly from this short introduction to the analytical approach to Economics which contrasted with the didactic and scholastic method of teaching of Economics in his Alma Mater. Six years later he sent one of his first publications to Pigou who wrote a charming note drawing attention to his treatment of the same subject in *A Study in Public Finance* and remarking rather pathetically that "he was now a mere vegetable".

Peacock graduated with First Class Honours in Economics and Political Science in 1947 and, with a wife and two children to support, was glad to accept a Lectureship at his Alma Mater. He believes that he obtained this post mainly because the other members of the Political Economy department were keen golfers, and a non-golfer had to be found to cover the lecture period on Wednesdays when golf competitions took place. Looking for experience elsewhere, his wife drew his attention to an advertisement for a Lectureship in Economics at the London School of Economics. The interviewing board included Phelps Brown, von Hayek, Meade and Robbins who asked a series of penetrating questions to which the candidate believes there are no answers; but he survived the ordeal and joined the London School of Economics in October 1948.

LSE presented a great challenge but also a splendid opportunity to Peacock. The challenge lay in adapting to the perception of Economics as an analytical discipline with important practical applications, whereas what training he had undergone had emphasised a scholarly interest in the economics classics. The opportunity lay in being brought into contact with the prominent figures in Economics already mentioned, from whom there was not only much to learn but also kindly encouragement. Within three years, after publishing a number of articles mainly on the economics of social policy, the post of Reader in Public Finance fell vacant, and he succeeded to a post once held by Hugh Dalton. It was typical of LSE to appoint a young man to be "thrown in at the deep end", and Peacock had to work hard to master a subject in which he had not previously specialised, although he had served an informal apprenticeship with Frank Paish, Professor of Business Finance, in writing policy memoranda on fiscal matters for the Liberal party. The visit to the United States which consolidated his growing interest in public expenditure is described in the First Lecture. The growth in public expenditure, particularly social expenditure, had become an important public issue in the UK, and Peacock's interest in policy questions led naturally to study of the reasons for its growth. The close, continuous and almost obsessive intellectual discourse in LSE encouraged collaboration in scientific work, and many of Peacock's contributions were the result of joint production, notably with Harold Edey, Louden Ryan, Frank Paish and later Jack Wiseman. He was also closely involved with graduate teaching and found time also to pursue a deep interest in music as conductor of the LSE orchestra. His presentation of a concert version of *L'Elisir D'Amore*, then practically unknown in the United Kingdom, was a proud moment! (Several of the participants in that venture have now become Professors of Economics, International Relations, History and Economic History!)

Peacock's expectations in 1956 amounted to the prospect that, after some years, he might obtain a personal professorship at LSE, but in May of that year he received an invitation to succeed Sir Alexander Gray as Professor of Commercial and Political Economy and Mercantile Law at the University of Edinburgh which carried with it the Headship of the Department of Political Economy. It was a difficult decision to make for it required him to return to general economics teaching and to shoulder a considerable administrative burden; and he was not yet thirty-four. The attractions of returning to Scotland overcame other considerations and he took over the post in January 1957.

He found that he had a fight on his hands in trying to appoint the number and type of staff commensurate with the formidable teaching and research burden, and in persuading existing staff that such changes were necessary. By his own reckoning he had neither the patience nor the skill to convince the University that the Department was grossly understaffed. He derived some consolation from publishing (after a long period of gestation) *The Growth of Public Expenditure in the United Kingdom* (with Jack Wiseman) alongside many professional articles, from having some very good graduate and undergraduate students, from demands to serve on Government inquiries, and from involvement with the Institute of Economic Affairs (IEA) and in international bodies concerned with public finance, notably the International Institute of Public Finance and the journal *Public Finance*. However, it took comparatively little persuading to induce him to accept an invitation, originating with Lionel Robbins, to be the first Professor appointed to the newly-founded University of York. He departed for York in the summer of 1962; he was forty years of age.

Peacock was determined to make York a major centre for the study of public economics within a period of ten years. To the extent that he was successful, it is because he was given the financial resources and *carte blanche* in recruitment of senior staff, which enabled him to appoint a preponderance of economists with an interest in public economics, though they were obliged to teach, and to an advanced level, in other fields. His efforts were complemented by those of his collaborator, Jack Wiseman, who joined him from LSE as first head of the Institute of Social and Economic Research. Together they founded what is now known as the "York School" and scholars and graduate students joined it from all parts of the world, but notably from Italy.

Although burdened with a considerable administrative load, as he was also Deputy Vice Chancellor in York's early years, he found time to continue writing with a developing interest in fiscal policy; to spend six fruitful months in Italy at the Fondazione Luigi Einaudi, Turin (1970), at the instigation of Francesco Forte; to engineer some much-needed reforms in the organisation of the conferences of the International Institute of Public Finance of which he was President (1966-1969); to Chair a Committee on the Finance of Britain's Orchestras (1969-1970) and to be a member of the Royal Commission on the Constitution (1971-1973). Although he remained a Professor of York until 1977, his three-year full-time appointment as Chief Economic Adviser of the Department of Trade and Industry (1973-1976) meant that he remained as Head of Department of Economics in name only after 1973.

The growth of the public sector was not only a source of detailed study by Peacock, but the cause of considerable anxiety to him. In the 1960s, he and Jack Wiseman acquired the reputation of being "radical reactionaries" because of their proposals for the reform of the finance of the welfare state so as to provide more scope for individual choice and initiative. Peacock's own direct experience as a senior government economist only confirmed his view that "market failure" could be matched by "collective failure" – a point elaborated at a more abstract level in his book with Charles Rowley on *Welfare Economics*. A proposal that he should join the only private university institution in the United Kingdom – the University College of Buckingham – and succeed Max (later Lord) Beloff as its Principal had a strong appeal and he left York, with much regret, in January 1978. His colleagues were understandably incredulous for this new private college had few resources, would have to depend on private finance and was not likely to achieve public recognition under a hostile government.

Buckingham had a hard struggle for academic recognition and financial independence, though it had dedicated academic and lay supporters. The chance to go for full university status came in 1979 with the appointment of the first Thatcher government. From then on students obtained some state grants, could obtain graduate employment in government institutions, and, finally, in 1983 Buckingham was granted full university status after Peacock had led a carefully orchestrated campaign with the support of the College's Council and academic advisory bodies. That task having been completed, Peacock, now sixty-two, decided to decline the offer of a further five years as Vice

Chancellor and to retire from a full-time academic and administrative appointment. His academic and public work had been recognised by honorary degrees from Stirling University (1974), which he had helped to found, and Zurich University (1984). Buckingham followed suit by marking him a Professor Emeritus and Doctor of Science (h.c.) in 1986. He had been elected a Fellow of the British Academy (FBA) in 1979.

At the time of delivering the Raffaele Mattioli Lectures, Peacock had returned to live in Scotland, with a part-time Research Professorship in Public Finance at Heriot-Watt University. His expectations of devoting himself to writing on the economics of public policy were only partly fulfilled. He had been closely involved at Buckingham in advising on government proposals to finance schools through an educational voucher system, but the proposal met fierce opposition in the Department of Education and Science and was abandoned. He had also been a special adviser on the future of the state retirement system, and helped to formulate proposals to offer a privatised system as an option and to reduce the compulsory element in earnings-related pensions. These proposals were embodied in new social security legislation. However, he had only been back in Edinburgh a few weeks when he was asked to Chair the Committee on the Future Financing of the British Broadcasting Corporation and the temptation to formulate radical proposals for the future financing and regulation of broadcasting was too tempting. The report of the Committee, with its emphasis on devising a broadcasting system which promoted the interests of the consumer, was regarded as highly controversial but it has become the point of departure for most of the Government's own proposals for reform. His record of public service was recognised by the award of a Knighthood in June 1987.

His major present preoccupation is the promotion of discussion on national and international economic policy issues but from a base outside London where most of the major policy institutes are concentrated. Hence the foundation of The David Hume Institute of which he is at present Executive Director. He is also at present Chairman of the Scottish Arts Council which allocates government funding to the performing arts in Scotland. He has always had a practical interest in music, and studied composition with the distinguished Austrian composer, Hans Gal. Just prior to the delivery of the Raffaele Mattioli Lectures, Peacock published his first musical composition – a set of "Waltz Contrasts" for pianoforte!

The Raffaele Mattioli Lectures are Peacock's attempt to crystallise his ideas on the scope and method of public choice analysis. He hopes that they form the point of departure for further studies with which he may also have the opportunity to enjoy, as he has always done, the occasional collaboration of colleagues. He claims that his days of close involvement in government policy are over and, at sixty-seven year of age, married for forty-five years and settled in one of the most beautiful cities in Europe, he would be content to become much less familiar with airport lounges and mainline railway stations.

2. Bibliography

Books, Monographs and Pamphlets

The Economics of National Insurance, London and Edinburgh: William Hodge, 1952.

National Income and Social Accounting (with Harold C. EDEY), London: Hutchinson, 1954 (Japanese and Portuguese editions).

The National Income of Tanganyika 1952-54 (with Douglas G. M. DOSSER), London: Her Majesty's Stationery Office, 1958.

The Growth of Public Expenditure in the United Kingdom (with Jack WISEMAN), Princeton: Princeton University Press and Oxford: Oxford University Press, 1961; Revised edition, London: George Allen and Unwin, 1967.

Analytical Concepts of Fiscal Policy with Special Reference to Developed Countries, Lisbon: Centro de Estudios de Estatistica Economica, 1962.

Education for Democrats (with Jack WISEMAN), London: Institute of Economic Affairs, 1964.

The Welfare Society, Unservile State Papers No. 2, 1961; Revised edition, 1966.

Educational Finance: Its Sources and Uses in the United Kingdom (with Howard GLENNERSTER and Robert LAVERS), Edinburgh and London: Oliver and Boyd, 1968.

Economic Aspects of Student Unrest (with Anthony J. CULYER), London: Institute of Economic Affairs, 1968.

Fiscal Policy and the Employment Problem in Less Developed Countries (with G. K. SHAW), Paris: Organization for Economic Co-operation and Development, 1971.

The Economic Theory of Fiscal Policy (with G. K. SHAW), London: George Allen and Unwin, 1971; Second edition, 1976 (Italian edition, 1972; Spanish edition, 1974).

The Political Economy of Public Spending, 1971, Mercantile Credit Lecture, Reading: University of Reading, 1972.

The Oil Crisis and the Professional Economist, Ellis Hunter Memorial Lecture, York: University of York, 1974.

Welfare Economics: A Liberal Restatement (with Charles K. ROWLEY), London: Martin Robertson, 1975 (Japanese edition, 1977).

The Composer in the Marketplace (with Ronald WEIR), London: Faber Music, 1975.

The Credibility of Liberal Economics, Seventh Wincott Memorial Lecture, London: Institute of Economic Affairs, 1977.

The Economic Analysis of Government and Related Themes, Oxford: Martin Robertson, 1979.

The Public Sector Borrowing Requirement (with G. K. SHAW), Buckingham: Buckingham University College, 1981.

Too Many Town Hall Staff? (with Martin RICKETTS), Report for the Federation of Civil Engineering Contractors, London: 1982.

Inflation and the Performed Arts (with Eddie SHOESMITH and Geoffrey MILLNER), London: Arts Council of Great Britain, 1983.

The Political Economy of Pension Provision (with Norman BARRY), Edinburgh: The David Hume Institute, 1986.

Making Sense of Broadcasting Finance, Robbins Lecture, Stirling: University of Stirling, 1986.

Economic Freedom and Modern Libertarian Thinking, Fulvio Guerrini Lecture, Torino: Centro di ricerca e documentazione «Luigi Einaudi», 1986.

David Hume in unserer Zeit: Vade Mecum zu einem frühen Klassiker (with Ernst TOPPITCH), Düsseldorf: Verlagsgruppe Handelsblatt, 1987.

Cultural Economics and the Finance of the Arts, Esmée Fairbairn Lecture, Lancaster: University of Lancaster, 1988.

The Trials of Setting Up in the University Business and the Funding Problem, Melbourne: La Trobe University, 1989.

Governments and Small Business (with Graham BANNOCK), London: Chapman, 1989.

Edited Works and Translations

Theory of the Market Economy, Translation of *Grundlagen der theoretischen Volkswirtschaftslehre* by Heinrich von STACKELBERG, Edinburgh and London: William Hodge, 1952.

Income Redistribution and Social Policy (editor, and co-author of Chapter 5 with P. R. BROWNING), London: Jonathan Cape, 1954.

Classics in the Theory of Public Finance (co-editor with Richard A. MUSGRAVE), London: Macmillan, 1958.

Public Expenditure: Appraisal and Control (co-editor with D. J. ROBERT-SON and author of Chapter 1), Edinburgh: Oliver and Boyd, 1963.

Government Finance and Economic Development (co-editor, and co-author of Chapter 14 with Gerald HAUSER), Paris: Organization for Economic Co-operation and Development, 1965.

Public Finance as an Instrument of Economic Development (editor, and author of Chapter 1), Paris: Organization for Economic Co-operation and Development, 1965.

Quantitative Analysis in Public Finance (editor, author of Chapter 1, and co-author of Chapter 8 with Elliot R. MORSS), New York: Praeger, 1969.

Structural Economic Policies in West Germany and the United Kingdom (editor, and author of various chapters), London: Anglo-German Foundation, 1980.

The Political Economy of Taxation (co-editor, and co-author of Chapter 1 with Francesco FORTE), Oxford: Blackwell, 1981.

The Regulation Game: How British and West German Firms Bargain with Government (editor and contributor), Oxford: Blackwell, 1984.

Public Expenditure and Government Growth (co-editor and contributor with Francesco FORTE), Oxford: Blackwell, 1985.

Germany's Social Market Economy: Origins and Evolution (co-editor, and co-author of Chapter 1 with Hans WILLGERODT), London: Macmillan, 1989.

German Neo-Liberals and the Social Market Economy (co-editor, and co-author of Chapter 1 with Hans WILLGERODT), London: Macmillan, 1989.

Contribution to Official Reports and Enquiries

Reform of Income Tax and Social Security Payments, Report of the Committee set up by the Liberal Party Organization (member), London: 1950.

Report of the Commission of Enquiry into the Natural Resources and Population Trends of the Colony of Fiji (member), Legislative Council of Fiji Council Paper No. 1, Suva, Fiji: 1960.

A Survey of Education within the Framework of Social and Economic Development in Afghanistan (member of Mission and contributor), Paris:

United Nations Educational, Scientific and Cultural Organization, 1962.

Report of the Committee on the Generation and Distribution of Electricity in Scotland (member), London: Her Majesty's Stationery Office, 1962.

Report of the Committee on the Impact of Rates (member: Allen Committee), London: Her Majesty's Stationery Office, 1965.

Report of the Royal Commission on Health of the Government of Newfoundland and Labrador, vol. 3, Appendix: 'The Economic and Financial Implications of an Expansion of Medical Services in Newfoundland', October 1966.

Report of the Presidential Fiscal Reform Commission of the Government of Colombia (member: Musgrave Commission), Bogota: 1969.

The Economics of Public Expenditure and its Consequences for Parliamentary Control (with Jack WISEMAN), First Report for the Select Committee on Procedure, London: Her Majesty's Stationery Office, 1969.

Public Policy and the Scrutiny of Taxation (with Jack WISEMAN), Second Special Report for the Select Committee of Procedure, London: Her Majesty's Stationery Office, 1970.

Report of the Arts Council Enquiry into Orchestral Resources in Britain (chairman: Peacock Report), London: Arts Council of Great Britain, 1970.

How Entry into the Common Market May Affect Britain's Invisible Earnings (main contributor), Report submitted to the Committee on Invisible Exports by the Economists Advisory Group, London: July 1971.

Royal Commission on the Constitution 1969-73 (member, and co-signatory, with Lord Crowther-Hunt, of the *Memorandum of Dissent*), London: Her Majesty's Stationery Office, 1973.

The Reform of Social Security (adviser), vols. 1 and 2, London: Her Majesty's Stationery Office, 1985.

Report of the Committee on Financing the BBC (chairman), London: Her Majesty's Stationery Office, 1986.

Articles

'The Finance of the Welfare State: The Costs of British Social Services' (unsigned), *The Round Table*, June 1949, pp. 240-7.

'The National Insurance Funds', *Economica*, N.S., August 1949, pp. 228-42.

'The Finance of British National Insurance', *Public Finance*, No. 3, 1950, pp. 341-68.

'Recent German Contributions to Economics', *Economica*, N.S., May 1950, pp. 175-87.

'Keynesianische Nationalökonomie und Anti-Inflations-Politik', *Zeitschrift für die Gesamte Staatswissenschaft*, December 1950, pp. 610-22.

'National Insurance and Economic Policy', *The Banker*, December 1950, pp. 373-8.

'Alternative Presentations of the Social Accounts' (with Harold C. EDEY), *Accounting Research*, January 1951, pp. 41-51.

'A Note on the Theory of Income Redistribution' (with D. BERRY), *Economica*, N.S., February 1951, pp. 83-90.

'The Problem of Economic Power', Review article of Walter EUCKEN's *Unser Zeitalter der Misserfolge*, *Weltwirtschaftliches Archiv*, No. 1, 1952, pp. 1*-6*.

'Theory of Population and Modern Economic Analysis, I', *Population Studies*, November 1952, pp. 114-22.

'Public Finance and the Welfare State', *The Banker*, 1953.

'Malthus in the Twentieth Century', in David GLASS, ed., *Introduction to Malthus*, London: Watts & Co., 1953.

'Sur la théorie des dépenses publiques', *Économie appliquée*, April-June 1953, pp. 427-45.

'Social Security and Inflation: A Study of the Economic Effects of an Adjustable Pensions Scheme', *Review of Economic Studies*, vol. 20, No, 3, 1953, pp. 169-73.

'Wage Claims and the Pace of Inflation (1948-51)' (with W. J. L. RYAN), *Economic Journal*, June 1953, pp. 385-92.

'Politique fiscale et budget national en Grande-Bretagne', *Revue de Science et de Législation financières*, July-September 1953, pp. 418-35.

'The Hyperbarbarous Technology', *Westminster Bank Review*, November 1953, pp. 5-9.

'Theory of Population and Modern Economic Analysis, II', *Population Studies*, March 1954, pp. 227-37.

'The Economics of Pension Funds' (with F. W. PAISH), *Lloyds Bank Review*, October 1954, pp. 14-28.

'The Economics of Dependence, 1952-82' (with F. W. PAISH), *Economica*, N.S., November 1954, pp. 279-99.

'Economic Theory and the Concept of an Optimum Population', in J. B. CRAGG and N. W. PIRIE, eds., *The Numbers of Man and Animals*, Edinburgh: Oliver and Boyd, 1955, pp. 1-12.

'Neuere Entwicklungen in der Theorie der "Fiscal Policy"', *Finanzarchiv*, N.S., vol. 16, No. 2, 1955, pp. 294-308.

'The Public Finances of the United Kingdom in 1954 and 1955', *Finanzarchiv*, N.S., vol. 16, No. 2, 1955, pp. 341-50.

'Théorie moderne de l'incidence de l'impôt et securité sociale', *Revue de Science et de Législation financières*, April-June 1955, pp. 347-60.

'The Future of Government Expenditure', *District Bank Review*, June 1955, pp. 27-41.

'Das Finanz- und Steuersystem Grossbritanniens', in Wilhem GERLOFF and Fritz NEUMARK, eds., *Handbuch der Finanzwissenschaft*, Second edition, vol. 3, Tübingen: Mohr (Paul Siebeck), 1956, pp. 212-35.

'The Finance of State Education in the United Kingdom' (with Jack WISEMAN), in *The Year Book of Education, 1956*, London: Evans Brothers, 1956, pp. 305-20.

'Tax Policy and the Budget 1956', *British Tax Review*, June 1956, pp. 65-73.

'A Note on the Balanced Budget Multiplier', *Economic Journal*, June 1956, pp. 361-5.

'The Savings-Investment Problem in Contemporary Britain', in *International Congress for the Study of Savings Problems*, Paris: Imprimerie Nationale, 1957.

'From Political Economy to Economic Science', Inaugural Lecture as Professor of Economic Science, University of Edinburgh, *University of Edinburgh Gazette*, 1957.

'Welfare in the Liberal State' (unsigned), in George WATSON, ed., *The Unservile State: Essays in Liberty and Welfare*, London: George Allen and Unwin, 1957, pp. 113-30.

'The British Budget for 1957-58', *Finanzarchiv*, N.S., vol. 18, No. 1, 1957, pp. 138-46.

'Sozialpolitik in Liberaler Sicht', *Schweizer Monatshefte*, March 1957.

'Production Functions and Population Theory', Review article, *Population Studies*, March 1957, pp. 298-305.

'L'économiste dans la littérature', *Revue de Science financière*, April-June 1957, pp. 192-201.

'The Economics of National Superannuation', *Three Banks Review*, September 1957, pp. 3-22.

'Some Observations on the Reports of the Royal Commission on the Taxation of Profits and Income', *National Tax Journal*, September 1957, pp. 255-65.

'Input-Output Analysis in an Underdeveloped Country: A Case Study' (with Douglas G. M. DOSSER), *Review of Economic Studies*, October 1957, pp. 21-4.

'The British Budget for 1958-59', *Finanzarchiv*, N.S., vol. 19, No. 2, 1958, pp. 284-91.

'The Economic Writings of Frances Horner', *Scottish Journal of Political Economy*, February 1958, pp. 60-4.

'Fiscal Policy and the Composition of Government Purchases' (with I. G. STEWART), *Public Finance*, No. 2, 1958, pp. 135-44.

'Monetary Policy and Central Bank Organization', *Scottish Bankers Magazine*, May 1958, pp. 3-11.

'The Government as an Employer' (with Thomas L. JOHNSTON), *Westminster Bank Review*, August 1958, pp. 6-10.

'Eine Analyse der Britischen Entwicklung aum Wohlfahrtstaat', *IFO-Studien*, vol. 5, No. 122, 1959.

'Politique économique et calcul du revenue national spécialement dans les pays sous-développés', *Revue de Science financière*, January-March 1959, pp. 35-48.

'The Public Sector and the Theory of Economic Growth', *Scottish Journal of Political Economy*, February 1959, pp. 1-12.

'The Rehabilitation of Classical Debt Theory', *Economica*, May 1959, pp. 161-66.

'Regional Input-output Analysis and Government Spending' (with Douglas G. M. DOSSER), *Scottish Journal of Political Economy*, November 1959, pp. 229-36.

'Built-in Flexibility and Economic Growth', in Gottfried BOMBACH, ed., *Stabile Preise in wachsender Wirtschaft*, Tübingen: Mohr (Paul Siebeck), 1960.

'The Government as a Buyer', *Purchasing Journal*, January 1960.

'The New Attack on Localized Unemployment' (with Douglas G. M. DOSSER), *Lloyds Bank Review*, January 1960, pp. 17-28.

'Les dépenses gouvernementales et la structure du marché', *Revue de Science financière*, January-March 1961, pp. 32-44.

'The International Distribution of Income, 1949 and 1957' (with Suphan ANDIC), *Journal of the Royal Statistical Society*, Series A (General), No. 2, 1961, pp. 206-18.

'The Past and Future of Public Spending' (with Jack WISEMAN), *Lloyds Bank Review*, April 1961, pp. 1-20.

'Economic Problems of a Multi-racial Society – The Fiji Case', *Scottish Journal of Political Economy*, October 1961, pp. 233-45.

'Stabilization and Planning in African Countries' (with Douglas G. M. DOSSER), *Public Finance*, No. 3, 1962, pp. 235-59.

'The Control and Appraisal of Public Investment in the United Kingdom', *Finanzarchiv*, N.S., September 1962, pp. 79-91.

'Economic Advice to Government in the United Kingdom', in Erwin von BERKERATH and Herbert GIERSCH, eds., *Probleme der normativen Ökonomik und der wirtschaftpolitischen Beratung*, Berlin: Duncker und Humblot, 1963.

'Monetary and Fiscal Policy in Relation to African Development', in E.A.G. ROBINSON, ed., *Economic Development for Africa South of the Sahara*, Proceedings of a Conference held by the International Economic Association, London: Macmillan, 1963, pp. 654-76.

'Economic Analysis and Government Expenditure Control', *Scottish Journal of Political Economy*, February 1963, pp. 1-16.

'Economic Growth and the Demand for Qualified Manpower', *District Bank Review*, June 1963, pp. 3-18.

'Economics of a Net Wealth Tax for Britain', *British Tax Review*, November-December 1963, pp. 388-99.

'Problems of Government Budgetary Reform', *Lloyds Bank Review*, January 1964, pp. 20-34.

'The International Distribution of Income with "Maximum" Aid' (with Douglas G. M. DOSSER), *Review of Economics and Statistics*, November 1964, pp. 432-4.

'The Political Economy of Social Welfare', *Three Banks Review*, December 1964, pp. 3-21.

'Towards a Theory of Inter-Regional Fiscal Policy', *Public Finance*, Nos. 1-2, 1965, pp. 7-17.

'Economic Growth and the Principles of Educational Finance in Developing Countries' (with Jack WISEMAN), in *Financing of Education for Economic Growth*, Paris: Organization for Economic Co-operation and Development, 1966.

'The Economics of Taxing Advertising', *Accountancy*, March 1966, pp. 160-3.

'The Social Accounting of Education' (with Robert LAVERS), *Journal of the Royal Statistical Society*, Series A (General), vol. 129, No. 3, 1966, pp. 448-66.

'Fiscal Surveys and Economic Development' (with Suphan ANDIC), *Kyklos*, No. 4, 1966, pp. 620-41.

'A Conceptual Scheme for the Analysis of Data on Educational Finance', in *Methods and Statistical Needs for Educational Planning*, Paris: Organization for Economic Co-operation and Development, 1967.

'Consumption Taxes and Compensatory Finance' (with John WILLIAMSON), *Economic Journal*, March 1967, pp. 27-45.

'Measuring the Efficiency of Government Expenditure' (with Jack WISEMAN), in A. R. PREST, ed., *Public Sector Economics*, Manchester: Manchester University Press, 1968, pp. 37-67.

'Stability, Growth and Budgetary Planning', in *The Budget Today*, Bruges: St Catherine's Press, 1968.

'The New Doctor's Dilemma' (with Robin SHANNON), *Lloyds Bank Review*, January 1968, pp. 26-38.

'Public Patronage and Music: An Economist's View', *Three Banks Review*, March 1968, pp. 1-19.

'The Welfare State and the Redistribution of Income' (with Robin SHANNON), *Westminster Bank Review*, August 1968, pp. 30-46.

'Welfare Economics and Public Subsidies to the Arts', *Manchester School*, December 1969, pp. 323-35.

'Justifying the Subsidy', *Opera*, May 1969, pp. 376-81.

'Public Expenditure as a Source of Finance for Medical Care in Britain' (with Jack WISEMAN), Appendix B in *Health Services Financing*, London: British Medical Association, 1970.

'Invisible Earnings' (with R. A. COOPER), in John PINDER, ed., *The Economics of Europe: What the Common Market Means for Britain*, London: Knight, 1971, pp. 169-82.

'Public Expenditure Research at the University of York', *Openbare Uitgaven*, June 1971.

'Fiscal Measures to Improve Employment in Developing Countries: A Technical Note' (with G. K. SHAW), *Public Finance*, No. 3, 1971, pp. 409-18.

'The Public Finance of Inter-Allied Defence Provision', in Ernesto D'ALBERGO, ed., *Studi "in memoriam" di Antonio De Viti de Marco*, Bari: Cacucci, 1972, pp. 371-84.

'Fiscal Means and Political Ends', in Maurice PESTON and Bernard CORRY, eds., *Essays in Honour of Lord Robbins*, London: Weidenfeld and Nicolson, 1972, pp. 82-98.

'New Methods of Appraising Government Expenditure: An Economic Analysis', *Public Finance*, No. 2, 1972, pp. 85-91.

'Pareto-Optimality and the Political Economy of Liberalism' (with Charles K. ROWLEY), *Journal of Political Economy*, May-June 1972, pp. 476-90.

'Welfare Economics and the Public Regulation of Natural Monopoly' (with Charles K. ROWLEY), *Journal of Public Economics*, August 1972, pp. 227-44.

'The Multiplier and the Valuation of Government Expenditures', *Finanzarchiv*, N. S., vol. 30, No. 3, 1972, pp. 418-23.

'Fiscal Measures to Improve Employment in Developing Countries: A Reply' (with G. K. SHAW), *Public Finance*, No. 4, 1972, pp. 489-90.

'Cost-Benefit Analysis and the Political Control of Public Investment', in J. N. WOLFE, ed., *Cost Benefit and Cost Effectiveness: Studies and Analysis*, London: George Allen and Unwin, 1973, pp. 17-29.

'The Economic Value of Musical Composition', in Bernhard KULP and Wolfgang STUZEL, eds., *Beitrage zu einer Theorie der Sozialpolitik*, Berlin: Duncker und Humblot, 1973, pp. 11-27.

'Cultural Accounting' (with Christine GODFREY), *Social Trends*, No. 4, London: Her Majesty's Stationery Office, 1973.

'Welfare Economics and the Public Regulation of Natural Monopoly: A Reply' (with Charles K. ROWLEY), *Journal of Public Economics*, February 1973, pp. 97-100.

'An Economic Analysis of the British Tax Credit Proposals' (with Alan MAYNARD), in *IFS Conference on Proposals for a Tax-Credit System*, London: Institute for Fiscal Studies, March 1973, pp. 11-24.

'Fiscal Measures to Create Employment: The Indonesian Case' (with G. K. SHAW), *Bulletin for International Fiscal Documentation*, November 1973, pp. 443-54.

'The Treatment of Government Expenditure in Studies of Income Distribution', in Warren L. SMITH and John M. CULBERSTON, eds., *Public Finance and Stabilization Policy: Essays in Honor of Richard A. Musgrave*, Amsterdam: North-Holland, 1974, pp. 151-67.

'The Problems of Performing Arts and Economic Analysis', in Bing CHEN, ed., *Understanding Economics*, Boston: Little, Brown, 1974.

'The Economic Analysis of Negative Income Taxation' (with Alan MAYNARD), in A. J. CULYER, ed., *Economic Policies and Social Goals*, London: Martin Robertson, 1974, pp. 79-93.

'The Economics of Museums and Galleries' (with Christine GODFREY), *Lloyds Bank Review*, January 1974, pp. 17-28.

'International Linkage Models and the Public Sector' (with Martin RICKETTS), *Public Finance*, No. 3, 1975, pp. 289-312.

'Studying Economic Policy', Foreword in R. M. GRANT and G. K. SHAW, eds., *Current Issues in Economic Policy*, Oxford: Philip Allan, 1975, pp. 1-9.

'The Treatment of the Principles of Public Finance in *The Wealth of Nations*', in Andrew S. SKINNER and Thomas WILSON, eds., *Essays on Adam Smith,* Oxford: Clarendon Press, 1976, pp. 553-67.

'The Political Economy of Devolution: The British Case', in Wallace E. OATES, ed., *The Political Economy of Fiscal Federalism*, Lexington, Mass.: Heath, 1976.

'The "Output" of the London Orchestras 1966-75', *The Musical Times*, August 1976.

'The Political Economy of the "Dispersive Revolution"', *Scottish Journal of Political Economy*, November 1976, pp. 205-19.

'Educational Expenditure in Great Britain' (with Susan NEWMAN), in *Educational Expenditure in France, Japan and the United Kingdom*, Paris: Organisation for Economic Co-operation and Development, 1977, pp. 245-326.

'Giving Economic Advice in Difficult Times', *Three Banks Review*, March 1977, pp. 3-23.

'Stabilization and Distribution Policy', in Martin PFAFF, ed., *Grenzen der Umverteilung*, Berlin: Duncker und Humblot, 1978, pp. 91-103.

'Trade Unions and Economic Policy', in *Trade Unions: Public Goods or Public "Bads"?*, London: Institute of Economic Affairs, 1978, pp. 117-25.

'The Economics of Bureaucracy: An Inside View', in *The Economics of Politics*, London: Institute of Economic Affairs, 1978, pp. 117-28.

'The Growth of the Public Sector and Inflation' (with Martin RICKETTS), in Fred HIRSCH and John H. GOLDTHORPE, eds., *The Political Economy of Inflation*, London: Martin Robertson, 1978, pp. 117-36.

'Preserving the Past: An International Economic Dilemma', in Pio CARONI *et al.*, eds., *Nur Oekonomie is keine Oekeonomie*, Festschrift für B. M. Biucchi, Bern: Verlag Paul Haupt, 1978, pp. 305-14.

'Is Fiscal Policy Dead?' (with G. K. SHAW), *Banca Nazionale del Lavoro Quarterly Review*, June 1978, pp. 107-22.

'Do We Need to Reform Direct Taxes?', *Lloyds Bank Review*, July 1978, pp. 28-40.

'Combined Defence and International Economic Co-operation' (with Keith HARTLEY), *World Economy*, 1978, pp. 327-39.

'Public Expenditure Growth in Post-Industrial Society', in Bo GUSTAFSSON, ed., *Post-Industrial Society*, London: Croom Helm, 1979, pp. 80-95.

'Approaches to the Analysis of Government Expenditure Growth' (with Jack WISEMAN), *Public Finance Quarterly*, January 1979, pp. 3-23.

'The British Economy and Its Problems', in Richard ROSE, ed., *Britain: Progress or Decline?*, London: Macmillan, 1980.

'On the Anatomy of Collective Failure', *Public Finance*, No. 1, 1980, pp. 33-43.

'Inter-governmental Fiscal Relations in a Unitary State: The Example of the United Kingdom' (with Martin RICKETTS), in Fritz NEUMARK and Norbert ANDEL, eds., *Handbuch der Finanzwissenschaft*, third edition, Tübingen: Mohr (Paul Siebeck), 1981, vol. 4, pp. 54-68.

'Fiscal Theory and the "Market" for Tax Reform', in Karl W. ROSKAMP and Francesco FORTE, eds., *Reforms of Tax Systems*, Detroit, Ill.: Wayne State University Press, 1981, pp. 11-21.

'Model Building and Fiscal Policy: Then and Now', *Finanzarchiv*, N.S., vol. 39, No. 1, 1981, pp. 43-52.

'Government Expenditure and the "Radical" Left', *Journal of Economic Affairs*, April 1981, pp. 145-9.

'Fiscal Policy in a Monetarist's World: The British Case', *Report of the Proceedings of Thirty-Third Tax Conference*, Toronto: Canadian Tax Foundation, 1982, pp. 18-30.

'Controlli microeconomici e macroeconomici della spesa pubblica', *Einaudi notizie*, 1982.

'Tax Evasion and Tax Revenue Loss' (with G. K. SHAW), *Public Finance*, No. 2, 1982, pp. 269-78.

'The LSE and Post-War Economic Policy', *Atlantic Economic Journal*, March 1982, pp. 35-40.

'Is Tax Revenue Overstated?' (with G. K. SHAW), *Journal of Economic Affairs*, April 1982, pp. 161-3.

'Calculating the Revenue Loss from Evasion' (with G. K. SHAW), *Journal of Economic Affairs*, July 1982, pp. 222-6.

'Reducing Government Expenditure: A British View', in Herbert GIERSCH, ed., *Reassessing the Role of Government in the Mixed Economy*, Tübingen: Mohr (Paul Siebeck), 1983, pp. 1-24.

'Welfare Economics, Public Finance and Selective Aid Policies', in Fritz MACHLUP, Gerhard FELS and Hubertus MULLER-GROELING, eds., *Reflections on a Troubled World Economy: Essays in Honour of Herbert Giersch*, London: Macmillan, 1983, pp. 238-53.

'Public X-Inefficiency: Informational and Institutional Constraints', in Horst HANUSCH, ed., *Anatomy of Government Deficiencies*, Berlin: Springer, 1983, pp. 125-38.

'Mittelfristige Finanzpolitik in einer monetaristischen Welt – Das Beispiel Grossbritannien', *Zeitschrift für Wirtschaftspolitik*, No. 1, 1983.

'Education Voucher Schemes: Strong or Weak?', *Journal of Economic Affairs*, January 1983, pp. 113-16.

'The Disaffection of the Taxpayer', Presidential Address to the Atlantic Economic Society, *Atlantic Economic Journal*, March 1983, pp. 7-15.

'The Politics of Culture and the Ignorance of Political Scientists: A Reply to F. F. Ridley', *Journal of Cultural Economics*, June 1983, pp. 23-6.

'Preface' and 'Tax Sharing: The West German Example' (with Lesley WAKEFIELD), in Thomas WILSON, ed., *Fiscal Decentralisation*, London: Anglo-German Foundation, 1984, pp. 109-32.

'Economics, Inflation and the Performing Arts', in Hilda BAUMOL and William J. BAUMOL, eds., *Inflation and the Performing Arts*, New York: New York University Press, 1984, pp. 107-26.

'The Political Economy of Strukturpolitik: A Tribute to the German Council of Economic Experts', *Zeitscrift für die gesamte Staatswissenschaft*, June 1984, pp. 364-70.

'Privatisation in Perspective', *Three Banks Review*, December 1984, pp. 3-25.

'Disability Policy in the United Kingdom' (with M. J. M. McCROSTIE), in Robert H. HAVEMAN, Victor HALBERSTADT and Richard V. BURKHAUSER, eds., *Public Policy Towards Disabled Workers*, Ithaca, N.Y.: Cornell University Press, pp. 517-73.

'The Cost Disease: Analytical and Policy Aspects', in Mary Ann HENDON, James F. RICHARDSON and William S. HENDON, eds., *Bach and the Box: The Impact of Televison on the Live Arts*, Akron, Oh.: Association of Cultural Economics, 1985.

'Is there a Public Debt Problem in Developed Countries?', in Bernard P. HERBER, ed., *Public Finance and Public Debt*, Detroit, Mi.: Wayne State University Press, 1986, pp. 29-41.

'The Political Economy of Public Spending', in John BRISTOW and Declan McDONAGH, eds., *Public Expenditure: The Key Issues*, Dublin: Institute of Public Administration, 1986, pp. 42-61.

'Der Nationalökonom als Berater der Wirtschafts- und Finanzpolitik', Böhm Bawerk Lecture (Innsbruck), *Wirtschaftspolitische Blätter*, 1986.

'Buckingham's Fight for Independence', *Economic Affairs*, February-March 1986, pp. 22-5.

'Bargaining and the Regulatory System' (with Martin RICKETTS), *International Review of Law and Economics*, June 1986, pp. 3-16.

'Technology and the Political Economy of Broadcasting', *Intermedia*, November 1986.

'Some Gratuitous Advice to Fiscal Advisers', in Hans M. VAN DE KAR and Barbara L. WOLFE, eds., *The Relevance of Public Finance for Policy-Making*, Detroit, Mi.: Wayne State University Press, 1987, pp. 265-75.

Entries on 'Economic Freedom', 'Hugh Dalton', 'Carl Dietzel', 'Alexander Henderson' and 'Ursula Hicks', in John EATWELL, Murray

MILGATE and Peter NEWMAN, eds., *The New Palgrave: A Dictionary of Economics*, London: Macmillan, 1987.

'Markets, Competition and Public Intervention: A Short Manifesto', *Micros*, vol. 6, No. 1, 1987.

'Fernsehfinanzierung und Verbraucher', *Zeitschrift für Wirtschaftspolitik*, No. 2, 1987, pp. 113-23.

'Government Debt and Growth in Public Spending' (with Ilde RIZZO), *Public Finance*, No. 2, 1987, pp. 285-91.

'The Politics of Investigating Broadcasting Finance', *Royal Bank of Scotland Review*, March 1987, pp. 3-16.

'Staatsfinanzen und Staatsburger', in Horst ZIMMERMAN, ed., *Die Zukunft der Staatsfinanzierung: Marburger Forum Philippinum*, Stuttgart: Wissenschaftliche Verlagsgesellschaft, 1988, pp. 11-27.

'Economic Freedom and Modern Libertarian Thinking', *Lloyds Bank Annual Review*, vol. 2, 1988, pp. 37-50.

'An Economic Analysis of Economic Advice Giving', *Atlantic Economic Journal*, September 1988, pp. 1-10.

'Introduction: Some Methodological Questions', in Cento VELJANOWSKI, ed., *Reaganomics and After*, London: Institute of Economic Affairs, 1989, pp. XI-XX.

'The Future of Public Service Broadcasting', in Cento VELJANOWSKI, ed., *Freedom in Broadcasting*, London: Institute of Economic Affairs, 1989, pp. 51-62.

'The Rise and Fall of the Laffer Curve', in D. Bös and B. FELDERER, eds., *The Political Economy of Progressive Taxation*, Berlin and Heidelberg: Springer, 1989, pp. 25-40.

'Economic Analysis of Problems of Government Selective Aid' (with Martin RICKETTS), in Manfred NEUMANN and Karl W. ROSKAMP, eds., *Public Finance and the Performance of Enterprises*, Detroit, Mi.: Wayne State University Press, 1989, pp. 197-210.

INDEX

INDEX

RAFFAELE MATTIOLI LECTURES

RAFFAELE MATTIOLI FOUNDATION
Fondazione Raffaele Mattioli
per la Storia del Pensiero Economico

Published

RICHARD F. KAHN, *The Making of Keynes' General Theory* (First edition: May 1984; Japanese edition, Tokyo: Iwanami Shoten, Publishers, April 1987).

FRANCO MODIGLIANI, *The Debate over Stabilization Policy* (First edition: July 1986).

CHARLES P. KINDLEBERGER, *Economic Laws and Economic History* (First edition: December 1989; Italian edition, Bari: Laterza, 1990; Spanish edition, Barcelona: Editorial Crítica, December 1990).

ALAN PEACOCK, *Public Choice Analysis in Historical Perspective* (First edition: March 1992).

To be published

ERIK F. LUNDBERG, *The Development of Swedish and Keynesian Macroeconomic Theory and its Impact on Economic Policy.*

NICHOLAS KALDOR, *Causes of Growth and Stagnation in the World Economy.*

SHIGETO TSURU, *Institutional Economics Revisited.*

RICHARD STONE, *Some British Empiricists in the Social Sciences.*

KARL BRUNNER - ALLAN H. MELTZER, *Money and the Economy. Issues in Monetary Analysis.*

DESIGN, MONOTYPE COMPOSITION AND PRINTING
BY STAMPERIA VALDONEGA, VERONA
MARCH MCMXCII